Medicine

Opposing Viewpoints®

Other Books of Related Interest

Medicine

Opposing Viewpoints®

Laura K. Egendorf, *Book Editor*

Daniel Leone, *President*
Bonnie Szumski, *Publisher*
Scott Barbour, *Managing Editor*

San Diego • Detroit • New York • San Francisco • Cleveland
New Haven, Conn. • Waterville, Maine • London • Munich

For more information, contact
Greenhaven Press
27500 Drake Rd.
Farmington Hills, MI 48331-3535
Or you can visit our Internet site at http://www.gale.com

LIBRARY OF CONGRESS CATALOGING-IN-PUBLICATION DATA
Medicine / Laura K. Egendorf, book editor.
p. cm. — (Opposing viewpoints)
Includes bibliographical references and index.
ISBN 0-7377-1234-1 (lib. bdg. : alk. paper) —
ISBN 0-7377-1233-3 (pbk. : alk. paper)
I. Egendorf, Laura K., 1973– II. Series.
R131 .M4167 2003
610—dc21   2002066460

"Congress shall make
no law...abridging the
freedom of speech, or of
the press."

First Amendment to the U.S. Constitution

The basic foundation of our democracy is the First
Amendment guarantee of freedom of expression.
The Opposing Viewpoints Series is dedicated to the
concept of this basic freedom and the idea that it is
more important to practice it than to enshrine it.

Contents

Why Consider Opposing Viewpoints?

"The only way in which a human being can make some
approach to knowing the whole of a subject is by hearing
what can be said about it by persons of every variety of
opinion and studying all modes in which it can be looked
at by every character of mind. No wise man ever
acquired his wisdom in any mode but this."

John Stuart Mill

In our media-intensive culture it is not difficult to find differing opinions. Thousands of newspapers and magazines
and dozens of radio and television talk shows resound with
differing points of view. The difficulty lies in deciding which
opinion to agree with and which "experts" seem the most
credible. The more inundated we become with differing
opinions and claims, the more essential it is to hone critical
reading and thinking skills to evaluate these ideas. Opposing
Viewpoints books address this problem directly by presenting stimulating debates that can be used to enhance and
teach these skills. The varied opinions contained in each
book examine many different aspects of a single issue. While
examining these conveniently edited opposing views, readers
can develop critical thinking skills such as the ability to
compare and contrast authors' credibility, facts, argumenta-
tion styles, use of persuasive techniques, and other stylistic
tools. In short, the Opposing Viewpoints Series is an ideal
way to attain the higher-level thinking and reading skills so
essential in a culture of diverse and contradictory opinions.

In addition to providing a tool for critical thinking, Opposing Viewpoints books challenge readers to question their
own strongly held opinions and assumptions. Most people
form their opinions on the basis of upbringing, peer pressure, and personal, cultural, or professional bias. By reading
carefully balanced opposing views, readers must directly
confront new ideas as well as the opinions of those with
whom they disagree. This is not to simplistically argue that

everyone who reads opposing views will—or should—change his or her opinion. Instead, the series enhances readers' understanding of their own views by encouraging confrontation with opposing ideas. Careful examination of others' views can lead to the readers' understanding of the logical inconsistencies in their own opinions, perspective on why they hold an opinion, and the consideration of the possibility that their opinion requires further evaluation.

Evaluating Other Opinions

To ensure that this type of examination occurs, Opposing Viewpoints books present all types of opinions. Prominent spokespeople on different sides of each issue as well as well-known professionals from many disciplines challenge the reader. An additional goal of the series is to provide a forum for other, less known, or even unpopular viewpoints. The opinion of an ordinary person who has had to make the decision to cut off life support from a terminally ill relative, for example, may be just as valuable and provide just as much insight as a medical ethicist's professional opinion. The editors have two additional purposes in including these less known views. One, the editors encourage readers to respect others' opinions—even when not enhanced by professional credibility. It is only by reading or listening to and objectively evaluating others' ideas that one can determine whether they are worthy of consideration. Two, the inclusion of such viewpoints encourages the important critical thinking skill of objectively evaluating an author's credentials and bias. This evaluation will illuminate an author's reasons for taking a particular stance on an issue and will aid in readers' evaluation of the author's ideas.

It is our hope that these books will give readers a deeper understanding of the issues debated and an appreciation of the complexity of even seemingly simple issues when good and honest people disagree. This awareness is particularly important in a democratic society such as ours in which people enter into public debate to determine the common good. Those with whom one disagrees should not be regarded as enemies but rather as people whose views deserve careful examination and may shed light on one's own.

Thomas Jefferson once said that "difference of opinion leads to inquiry, and inquiry to truth." Jefferson, a broadly educated man, argued that "if a nation expects to be ignorant and free . . . it expects what never was and never will be." As individuals and as a nation, it is imperative that we consider the opinions of others and examine them with skill and discernment. The Opposing Viewpoints Series is intended to help readers achieve this goal.

David L. Bender and Bruno Leone,
Founders

Greenhaven Press anthologies primarily consist of previously published material taken from a variety of sources, including periodicals, books, scholarly journals, newspapers, government documents, and position papers from private and public organizations. These original sources are often edited for length and to ensure their accessibility for a young adult audience. The anthology editors also change the original titles of these works in order to clearly present the main thesis of each viewpoint and to explicitly indicate the opinion presented in the viewpoint. These alterations are made in consideration of both the reading and comprehension levels of a young adult audience. Every effort is made to ensure that Greenhaven Press accurately reflects the original intent of the authors included in this anthology.

Introduction

"Today, there is no better nation in which to become sick than the United States."

—Doug Bandow

"Yes, as we're often told, American medicine is the best in the world. . . . But good as it is, it still could be a lot better."

—Daniel S. Greenberg

The American health care system is the most expensive per capita in the world, with annual health care costs per person of $4,187. Many argue that this sum is money well spent, but others insist that such an outlay does not always translate into the highest quality of medicine. Many people contend that the American medical system does not provide consistently high-quality health care. They maintain that the level of care could be improved if the United States adopted the single-payer health care plan used in Canada.

According to the World Health Organization (WHO), in its *World Health Report 2000*, the United States ranks thirty-seventh out of 191 health systems, ranking behind nations as varied as Belgium, Colombia, and Malta. One reason for the ranking is that WHO does not consider the American health care system to be financed fairly; for example, a poor person who spends the same amount of money on health care as someone who is wealthier will spend a greater percentage of his or her income on health care costs. Moreover, many Americans are left outside the system—44 million are uninsured. This high number of uninsured Americans can be attributed to the fact that Americans typically obtain health care through their employers. People whose employers do not provide health insurance, and those who are self-employed or unemployed, are more likely to be uninsured.

American doctors widely agree that the quality of care in the United States has declined. In a survey conducted in fall 2000 by Harvard University and the Commonwealth Fund, 56 percent stated that they believed "their ability to provide quality care has worsened in the past five years." Doctors also expressed concern about a shortage of nurses, medical errors, and the affordability of prescription drugs. The doctors contended that the level of care would improve if they could spend more time with patients.

In some cases, however, patients would not be well served by spending more time with their doctors. According to *Health Letter*, a publication of the Public Citizen Health Research Group, federal agencies and state medical boards disciplined 16,638 doctors between 1987 and 1996. The most serious offenses committed by these doctors include sexual abuse and misconduct, incompetent and negligent care, substance abuse, criminal conviction, and the overprescription and misprescription of drugs. The publication concludes: "This country's system for ensuring medical quality needs to be made much stronger. . . . Most states need to strengthen their medical practice statutes [and] restructure their medical boards." Another concern, raised by science journalist Daniel S. Greenberg, is that doctors too often order surgeries, particularly hysterectomies and bypass surgeries, whose medical benefit is uncertain. He also questions the need for new and costly medical technology: "The nasty secret of health care economics is that a lot done for patients is useless or dangerous, and costly, and that much that could help them, at relatively low cost, isn't done."

Critics of the American health care system assert that this nation should look north for a solution. In *History of Medicine: A Scandalously Short Introduction*, Jacalyn Duffin states, "The Canadian health care system is the envy of the Western world." Canada uses a "single-payer system" in which a single government fund within each province pays the physicians, hospitals, and health care providers. Thus the government, not employers, provides health insurance in Canada, and so all Canadians are covered. Advocates contend that all Americans would have health insurance and greater freedom of choice in doctors and hospitals under a single-payer system.

Despite criticisms of health care in the United States, numerous commentators and health care workers praise the successes of American medicine. Julie Chan, a research assistant at the Cato Institute, a libertarian public policy organization, questions the ranking criteria WHO used in its *World Health Report 2000*. She argues that the organization bases its conclusions on inaccurate and inconsistent data. However, even the World Health Organization is not wholly critical of the American medical system. WHO concludes in its report that the United States is unsurpassed regarding choice in providers, speed of response in emergencies, confidentiality of patient records, and respect for the dignity of individuals.

Doug Bandow, a senior fellow at the Cato Institute, cites advances in medical technology—which have helped the United States achieve a life expectancy rate of 77.26 years and an infant mortality rate of 6.76 deaths per 1,000 live births—as proof of the nation's excellent medical care. Among these scientific achievements are fetal surgeries, organ transplants, magnetic resonance imaging (MRIs), and gene therapy. Although the United States is not the only nation to take advantage of these new treatments and technologies, Bandow maintains that American medicine is superior to other nations because it rewards innovation and encourages competition.

Many commentators believe that there is no reason to follow Canada's lead and that the single-payer system is fraught with numerous problems. In an article for *Insight on the News*, Robert LeBow, former president of Physicians for a National Health Program, claims that despite the purported success of the Canadian system, many emergency rooms have closed and long waits for treatment are common. He also cites a 1999 poll that found that three out of every four Canadians believe that their health care system is in crisis. In addition, 59 percent of Canadian doctors expressed concerns about the quality of health care in Canada in the fall 2000 Harvard University survey. The quality of Canadian health care is also not consistent for all citizens. Political activist Stephen Gowans maintains that many services are no longer covered by the health system, leaving them available only to Canadians wealthy enough to pay out of pocket for them.

As the debate on the quality of health care in the United States suggests, the American medical system is one of the most scrutinized in the world. In *Medicine: Opposing View-*

points, the authors consider the breakthroughs and problems in American medicine in the following chapters: What Problems Confront American Medicine? Is Alternative Medicine Effective? Are New Medical Technologies Beneficial? What Is the Future of Medicine? In their viewpoints, the authors examine the state of the American medical system and what its future may hold.

CHAPTER 1

What Problems Confront American Medicine?

Chapter Preface

Medicine is often considered to be a lucrative and rewarding career. However, in recent years, the number of doctors and nurses has declined sharply. The shortage of medical professionals is one of many problems facing American medicine. Such a deficit is troubling because it can seriously affect the quality of health care. Because the remaining doctors and nurses are overworked, they are more likely to commit medical errors and will not have the time to give each patient individual attention.

Managed care is frequently cited as a reason for the physician shortage. The California Medical Association (CMA) reported in July 2001 that 43 percent of the doctors it surveyed said that they would retire within three years because they no longer wished to cope with increased regulations and low reimbursements from health maintenance organizations (HMOs). In an article for *Physician's News Digest*, doctor C. Richard Schott explained how managed care has had a detrimental effect on physicians. He contends, "Years of personal and family sacrifice and debt to train as physicians are now 'rewarded' by a lifetime of endless stressful hours of under-appreciated work including on-call time, compounded by constant fears of frivolous litigation, [and] endless manipulation by third party payers."

Managed care is also cited as one of many factors contributing to the nursing shortage. According to the American Hospital Association (AHA), nurses report dissatisfaction with their jobs due to the increased paperwork produced by managed care. The AHA reported that as many as 126,000 jobs for registered nurses were open in 2001. According to the AHA, other factors for the nursing shortage include a workforce populated with employees nearing retirement age, a decline in nursing school enrollment, and difficult and often exhausting responsibilities.

The shortage of qualified health care professionals is one problem confronting American medicine. In the following chapter, the authors consider some of the issues that affect the quality of the American medical system.

"*If patients are too sick and vulnerable,
health maintenance organizations
(HMOs) would prefer that they stay out of
their marketplace.*"

Health Maintenance Organizations Have Undermined American Medicine

Suzanne Gordon

Health maintenance organizations (HMOs) have compromised care of the sick, Suzanne Gordon maintains in the following viewpoint. Gordon claims that because HMOs allocate a small, fixed amount for each patient a doctor sees, doctors have begun viewing sicker patients as financial losses instead of people in need of compassionate care. According to Gordon, universal health care is the best way to ensure that sick people are treated properly. Gordon is a freelance journalist and author whose books include *Life Support: Three Nurses on the Front Lines*.

As you read, consider the following questions:
1. According to Gordon, how do "capitated" payments bankrupt physicians?
2. In Gordon's opinion, why is caring for ill people difficult?
3. How much does the United States spend per person on health care each year, as stated by the author?

A doctor I know [has] received a mail solicitation from a company that promised to help him manage managed care. The secret to success? Physicians need to learn how to pick the right patients—healthy people who rarely, if ever, visit their doctor—and shun the unprofitable sick.

Driving Doctors Out of Business

In the growing competition for health care market share, it is becoming clear that there is a group of customers the nation's managed care companies definitely don't want to attract. If patients are too sick and vulnerable, health maintenance organizations (HMOs) would prefer that they stay out of their marketplace.

One of the most effective ways to dump such patients is to drive the most ethical and compassionate physicians out of practice. An article in the *New England Journal of Medicine* explained why so many California physician groups are going bankrupt. Today, many HMOs use a system of "capitated" payments to control costs. Under capitation, physicians receive a small fixed rate per patient per month, no matter how sick the patient is and how much treatment and care he or she needs. Under this system, sick patients can literally bankrupt their physicians.

In Grand Rapids, Michigan, pediatrician Beatrice Murray and her three partners devoted part of their practice to caring for children paralyzed in accidents or suffering from metabolic diseases, cancer, cystic fibrosis, cerebral palsy and kidney failure. These children must take multiple medications, may have breathing or feeding tubes, often need frequent visits to the hospital and will be severely, chronically ill for the rest of their lives.

Over the years, the HMOs in Murray's area began to capitate her practice. With variations based only on sex and age rather than disease severity, all now pay fixed fees for all patients. Murray and her partners received from $6 to $30 per child per month to provide for all their out-patient needs.

To become more efficient, Murray's practice hired a nurse to help coordinate care. The doctors also scheduled longer visits to provide more comprehensive and, they hoped, less costly care. Patients and their parents loved these additional services. But this very customer satisfaction and loyalty was, as Murray puts it, "the knife to the heart" of her practice. Parents of sick children told the parents of other sick children about the practice. More sick children came as patients. All these satisfied customers were bankrupting the group.

An Exhausting Job

Under even the most generous health care system, caring for sick people is a difficult job. Doctors can't always figure out what's wrong with a sick patient and aren't always certain about the proper course of treatment. Even under the best of circumstances, sick people can be angry, afraid, irritable, in pain or denial and resistant to following their doctors' advice. This makes them a drain on the empathy of the most compassionate doctor.

Rall. © 1999 by Universal Press Syndicate. Reprinted with permission.

Add to this managed care micromanagement of every clinical decision and you have a recipe for turning the care of the sick from a difficult mission into an intolerable burden. Under the 1-800-Mother-May-I system of HMO utilization review, doctors must get pre-approval for every treatment they prescribe and action they take. To really care for their patients, they must spend hours on the phone arguing with insurance company bureaucrats.

After a while, many doctors just burn out. "A sick patient comes into my office, and I wonder how much time it will take to care for them," one doctor told me. Some physician practices refuse to fight insurance company denials of care for their patients. Some are unwilling to accept HMO patients and will take only those who can pay for their services out of pocket—a strategy that rewards HMOs and punishes the sick.

Pitting Doctors Against Patients

A recent PBS "Frontline" show about a group of physicians in Boston, "Dr. Solomon's Dilemma," chillingly documented just how HMOs turn physicians against the sick. HMOs now send physician groups weekly accountings of the cost of every pill a patient takes, test he receives, day in the hospital he uses or home care or physical therapy session he consumes. Any cost that is not covered by the increasingly parsimonious rates physicians receive for each patient comes directly out of the groups' coffers. Not surprisingly, doctors begin to view a patient who has diabetes or heart disease or cancer not just as a sick person who needs compassionate care but as a financial loss.

In a truly remarkable feat of financial alchemy, insurers and other advocates of market health care argue that there isn't enough money in the $1.2-trillion American health care system to care for the sick. The U.S. spends $4,600 per person per year on health care—four times as much as we do on national defense and twice as much as is spent by Western European nations, most of which have better health outcomes. A publicly coordinated universal system is the only way this country will ever save money on health care. As health care economists like Alan Sager at the Boston University School of Public Health have demonstrated, the administrative and clinical savings and cheaper drug prices that result are more than enough to buy care for everyone.

Which is why action on universal health care is increasing

at the state level. Legislative or ballot initiatives supporting universal health care are being considered in Massachusetts, Maryland and Washington. Also, U.S. Rep. John F. Tierney (D-Mass.) has introduced in Congress a bill that would encourage states to develop their own systems of universal care by removing federal regulatory obstacles and providing planning and implementation grants. [The bill did not reach the House floor. A ballot measure in Massachusetts failed in 2000. Measures in Maryland and Washington are being considered for 2002.]

Americans have a clear choice. We can continue using our premium dollars and taxes to finance an ever-increasing war against the sick. Or we can create a health care system that does what it's supposed to do: Keep us healthy as long as possible and then care for us when we get sick.

*"The overwhelming majority of Americans
find their HMOs good to excellent."*

Health Maintenance Organizations Have Improved American Medicine

Thomas W. Hazlett

In the following viewpoint, Thomas W. Hazlett claims that despite the crusade against managed care, health maintenance organizations (HMOs) have improved the quality and affordability of American medicine. He asserts that doctors' efforts to reduce the power of HMOs will result in an increase in medical insurance costs, which will make quality health care too expensive for many Americans. Hazlett is a resident scholar at the American Enterprise Institute, a think tank dedicated to preserving private enterprise and limiting the power of governments.

As you read, consider the following questions:
1. What was the medical cost inflation rate in 1991, as stated by the author?
2. According to Hazlett, what has resulted from doctors running up medical tabs?
3. In Hazlett's opinion, how does unaffordable health care cause illness?

D r. Ken Smith has a mission: to destroy the health maintenance organization (HMO) system which today enrolls 85 percent of insured Americans. The Boston-based physician's reasons are simple and humane: "We are for patients, not profits." And his disgust is real: "How dare somebody in some board room in Connecticut decide what I'm worth, and on a whim decide that my worth should be reduced?"

The elements of the current crusade against managed care combine the front-page horror story of the access-denied victim with the political clout of a network of influential millionaires. In swank country clubs all across the land, high-powered attorneys are burying the hatchet with prosperous physicians, getting beyond that little multibillion-dollar spat over medical malpractice. Now they're toasting martinis and swearing litigation against the common enemy: HMOs that clamp down on medical costs.

The Reason for Managed Care

It may shock the good Dr. Smith, but many of the common folk are quite used to having distant big shots in faraway boardrooms establish the price for their labor. And as for the purity of spirit to which Smith appeals, we do appreciate the thought. But it's best to avoid any kind of competition regarding who's been more successful in bringing health care to the masses, the typical HMO shareholder vs. the typical M.D. After all, who is more likely to be recreating out on the golf course Wednesday afternoon?

The health care market is tricky, and the shadow under which all discussion takes place is the cost explosion tied to third-party payments. When Dr. Smith was perfectly free to prescribe for "his" patient and push the costs onto others— well, that was the Golden Age for doctors. And, coincidentally, 9.9 percent annual medical cost inflation (just to pick the peak year, 1991) for the rest of us.

Managed care stepped in—indeed, it arrived in an ambulance answering a 911 call from ratepayers. HMOs had a tough job to do, teaching lots of doctors with egos the size of Smith's that there ain't no such thing as a free surgical procedure. They have yet to succeed; a group Smith has helped to organize, The Ad Hoc Committee to Defend

Health Care, protests the "HMO bean counters" and advocates a single-payer system.

The reality is that the rationing that accompanies state-run systems makes the HMOs look like big spenders. That's not because the government hires better "bean counters." Quite the reverse—the beans sort of just disappear. And then it's, "Sorry, you'll just have to wait on that heart bypass until some more beans turn up."

The Aim of Doctors

Marc Roberts, a Harvard economist specializing in health care markets, claims that the doctors' real aim is "to regain status, power and income that they lost in this for-profit industry," and that holding the patient's welfare out as a bargaining chip is a smart stratagem. "They wouldn't gain any support if they stood up and said, 'Instead of making $300,000, I now make $200,000, and you should all feel sorry for me." The blunt fact is that letting doctors run up medical tabs resulted in runaway expenditures, stealing money from the pockets of wage earners, who ultimately pay in the form of reduced take-home.

The Economic Benefits of Managed Care

Dr. Uwe Reinhardt: The best model you can think of in terms of employer-provided [health] insurance is parents who give their adolescents an open-ended credit card with no strings attached. But secretly every month they take what the kids bill to the card out of the kids' trust fund. Total compensation in the '80s went up, but take-home pay was flat. And the difference was all eaten up by health insurance. Most of the savings from managed care in the 1990s flowed back through the paychecks of workers, and that was a dramatic victory for the working man. So we economists believe that whatever you can say about the managed-care industry, it helped fatten the paychecks of workers' take-home pay in the '90s.

Uwe Reinhardt, as quoted by Scott Hensley, *Wall Street Journal*, February 21, 2001.

Unaffordability is itself a cause of illness, as it puts more Americans outside the health insurance system altogether, lessening their access to regular checkups and preventive medicine. Instead, they increasingly resort to visits to crowded hospital emergency rooms. Treatment there is inefficiently administered—and quietly tacked onto the bills of paying customers, further driving up costs and pushing more working people out. As consumers, many of us prefer plans which offer a wide range of choice among doctors and treatments. But to receive the benefits from that high-cost deal, we do—and should—pay more via higher premiums and lower reimbursements. Government surely has a role to play enforcing contracts with insurers who attempt to renege and as a smart shopper purchasing large volumes of health care directly. (My understanding is that neither courts nor Medicare and Medicaid are as yet perfectly administered.)

Ignoring Majority Opinion

The pressure to realistically assess the cost-benefit tradeoffs in medical care should be welcomed by those outside the fashionable salons where "for-profit" medicine is profitably denounced. In fact, the overwhelming majority of Americans find their HMOs good to excellent, and most rate them as superior to traditional health insurance on the value/dollar scale.

That's a state of affairs that the HMO reformers aim to change. Stuart Altman, professor of health policy at Brandeis University, notes: "The more we reduce the power of managed care to control spending by restricting services, the more we are going to take away the pressure on providers to constrain spending."

That's what doctors want, that's why lawyers will sue, and that's the reason Congress will legislate. But don't feel left out—you'll get the bill.

> "Health care institutions and individual
> caregivers continue to provide different
> care to their minority patients than they
> give to those who are white."

Racism Is a Problem in Modern Medicine

Sidney D. Watson

In the following viewpoint, Sidney D. Watson asserts that health care institutions and caregivers discriminate against minorities. According to Watson, minority Americans receive fewer preventive procedures, diagnostic tests, and other medical services than their white counterparts despite having similar insurance coverage. She contends that such disparities are medical errors that reflect America's history of racial segregation. Watson is a law professor at Saint Louis University who specializes in health law and health care access for the poor.

As you read, consider the following questions:
1. What must a plaintiff prove in order to win a malpractice suit, according to Watson?
2. What diseases affect minority Americans more frequently than white Americans, according to the author?
3. How does Watson define "race" and "ethnicity"?

Excerpted from "Race, Ethnicity, and Quality of Care: Inequalities and Incentives," by Sidney D. Watson, *American Journal of Law and Medicine*, Summer/Fall 2001. Copyright © 2001 by the American Journal of Law and Medicine. Reprinted with permission.

As was my custom, I moved from one exam room to the next with a fluidity that comes from years of practice, yet I was stopped in my tracks when Mr. North rose to his feet to greet me. His deep ebony, six foot-three-inch frame dwarfed my pale, five-foot-three presence. The tremendous hands on his 260-pound body grabbed my own outstretched right hand and shook it. . . . I glanced at his face, trying to see through my initial discomfort, only to be greeted by my own face staring back at me from the silver, reflective sunglasses he wore beneath a baseball cap that covered his head and any hair that might have been growing on it. His huge chest was tightly wrapped in a black T-shirt that, even in its largest version, couldn't stretch comfortably to encompass his pectoral girth. . . .

Mr. North became one of my favorite patients. . . . I like him because I realize how hard I have had to work all of my life to overcome the racist feelings that made me fear him when we first met and that never allow me to act completely naturally in his presence. [Neil S. Caiman, "Out of the Shadow," *Health Affairs*, 2000]

R ace matters. While Medicaid and Medicare have increased access to care for poor and minority Americans, they have not erased differences in the quality of care received by minorities, particularly poor minorities. Health care institutions and individual caregivers continue to provide different care to their minority patients than they give to those who are white. These treatment differentials have complex origins. Bias, prejudice, class and money all play a role. Nevertheless, differences based on race and ethnicity rather than medical need are medical mistakes.

Designing a Better Health Care System

This viewpoint uses the Institute of Medicine ("IOM") report on quality and safety in health care, *To Err Is Human: Building a Safer Health System*, as a template for thinking about race linked differentials in health care access and treatment. The theme of the IOM report is that efforts to improve quality of care should shift from blaming individuals for past errors to designing better systems to prevent future errors. Similarly, attempts to reduce race-based disparities in medical care need to move from a backward looking focus on blame to designing systems that assure patients get medical care based upon their medical need and preferences rather than care that is mis-colored by their race and ethnicity. Civil rights law has provided the legal framework for examining differentials in care for minority and poor people. Typically, civil rights enforcement, like malpractice litigation, focuses on identifying whom or what to blame. In malpractice, a plaintiff must establish the relevant standard of care, prove that the health care provider violated that standard and that the violation caused the patient's injury. In a civil rights case, blame is laid by proving the health care provider either intentionally discriminated or used policies, practices or procedures that, while not intended to discriminate, have an unjustified, disproportionate adverse impact on minority patients.

Civil rights litigation, like medical malpractice, can redress some race-based medical errors. However, racial disparities in medical treatment are the result of multiple, complicated, historically rooted factors that color—often in deeply subconscious ways—both patients' and providers' decisions. As such they are often not amenable to the proof format—and blame laying—required by civil rights laws. . . .

[This viewpoint] . . . [catalogues] the recent research documenting the different care provided to racial and ethnic minorities and confirming that these differentials are likely the result of a complicated mix of medical errors and mistakes rather than variations in patient need. . . .

Poorer Quality of Health Care

There is absolutely no doubt that Mr. North is treated differently than my white, middle-class patients. The echocardiography lab where he had an appointment sent him home because he was ten minutes late, having to stop every block to rest in the walk from his home to the hospital on a particularly windy day. The pharmacy refused to refill his insulin syringes without a written prescription, even though he had been getting them at the same pharmacy for the past two years. I try to help in every way I can. Every time I send him to a new consultant, I call ahead with an introduction. I tell them how smart Mr. North is, how compliant he is with every aspect of his treatment, and how he knows so much about his medical condition and the medications he takes. I hope that my introduction will enable them to see my patient as I see him now, not as I saw him the first time we met. He needs that help in order to get the medical care he requires and deserves. [G. Caiman]

Race matters. A plethora of studies and reports document that the patient's race makes a difference in the care received. Race and ethnicity are consistently linked with different and poorer patterns of health access and treatment.

The Effects of Institutional Racism

The current health disparity is the cumulative result of both past and current racism throughout the American culture. Because of institutional racism, minorities have less education and fewer educational opportunities; minorities are disproportionately homeless and have significantly poorer housing options; and minorities disproportionately work in low pay, high health risk occupations (i.e., migrant farm workers, fast food workers, garment industry workers). In addition, the institutional racism in health care affects access to health care and the quality of health care received. Despite efforts to eliminate discrimination and reduce racial segregation over the past 30 years, there has been little change in the quality of or access to health care for many minorities and women. Discrimination in health care delivery, financing, and research continues to exist.

Institute on Race, Health Care and the Law, "Racism and Racial Discrimination in the U.S. Health Care System," January 1, 2001.

Minority Americans have significantly higher rates of cancer, stroke, heart disease, AIDS, diabetes, and other severe health problems than white Americans. However, even though minority Americans are generally in worse health than white Americans, they have fewer doctor visits, receive less primary care and fewer preventive procedures even when they have the same insurance coverage. Insured Blacks and Hispanics are less likely than whites to have private physicians and are more likely than whites to rely on hospital emergency rooms and outpatient clinics for primary care. As a result, Black, Hispanic and Native Americans are hospitalized more often than whites.

Moreover, health care professionals provide different—and generally less—care to their minority patients. When hospitalized, African-Americans receive fewer surgical interventions, diagnostic tests, medical services, and less optimal interventions than whites—even when their diagnosis, symptoms, and source of payment are the same. The findings for African-Americans are consistent for every service studied: cardiology and cardiac surgery, obstetrics, general medicine, kidney transplants, hip replacements, mammograms, oncology and leg sparing surgery for peripheral vascular disease. All told, African-Americans get only about three-quarters the high technology interventions prescribed for whites. They are more likely to be discharged in an unstable condition and more likely to have longer hospital stays.

Outpatient care is no different. African-American patients are less likely to be prescribed antidepressants for major depression and anti-retroviral therapy for HIV infection. They are also less likely to get adequate treatment for cancer-related pain.

Treatment of Hispanics and Native Americans

While less is known about access and treatment for other minority Americans, the few available studies confirm that Hispanic and Native Americans suffer from similar treatment disparities. Both Hispanic and Native Americans are significantly less likely than whites to receive cardiac bypass surgery and angioplasty, and Hispanics are less likely to receive other major therapeutic procedures. Hispanics are also less likely to get adequate treatment for cancer-related pain, and are twice as likely as white patients to receive no pain medication when treated in the emergency room for bone fractures.

These race-based treatment differences raise concerns about the quality of medical care for minority Americans. They are not the result of biology, age, gender, clinical condition, severity of disease or insurance status. Contrary to popular belief, the gaps cannot be attributed to insurance status or income: significant differences exist even when these factors are controlled for. Although most studies merely document disparities in the rates of procedures based upon the patient's race and ethnicity, those that examine the actual quality of care provided to patients tend to confirm that minority patients not only receive less care, but poorer quality care.

Understanding America's Medical History

Thus, race-linked disparities signal some kind of error. Some may be mistakes in judgment—the result of a wrong belief or misapprehension about the disease or patient's race, ethnicity or class. Other disparities may be the result of ignorance, carelessness or oversight. Many are likely the result of poor communication. Some may be transgressions of law. All are colored by America's history of slavery and segregation. Minority patients do not always trust white caregivers or the medical care system. Caregivers may carry deep-seated, often unconscious stereotypes about patients of other races and ethnic groups. Class differences are likely to accentuate and complicate racial and ethnic differences. Cross cultural and cross-class communication can be difficult not only when the participants speak different languages, but even when they appear to share a tongue. Individual institutions and the health care system retain vestiges of a formerly segregated system that compound the problem. Residential and geographic segregation mean that health care providers do not locate their practices where large numbers of minority patients, particularly poor minority patients, live.

In America, race is not just a skin color, and ethnicity is not just culture. Race and ethnicity are social categories that reflect differential access to power and social resources. Throughout American history, law and custom have relegated minority groups to different—and inferior—treatment. Medical care is no exception.

"The charge of physician bias against minority patients is often made reflexively."

Racism Is Not a Problem in Modern Medicine

Sally Satel

In the following viewpoint, Sally Satel asserts that the American medical system does not discriminate against minorities. She contends that claims of bias ignore the actual reasons for any disparities in health care, such as some minority groups' unwillingness to undergo surgery or the frequency with which different minority groups develop certain diseases. Moreover, according to Satel, the underlying health of a patient and the procedures offered at the hospital at which he or she is treated also help determine patient options. Satel is a lecturer at the Yale University School of Medicine and the author of *PC, M.D.: How Political Correctness Is Corrupting Medicine*, from which the following viewpoint has been excerpted.

As you read, consider the following questions:
1. How were black patients and medical students treated in the 1960s, according to Satel?
2. According to the author, why is limb amputation more common among black patients?
3. How does a patient's clinical condition affect his or her doctor's treatment, as explained by Satel?

One evening in 1994 Dr. Pius K. Kamau was on call at his Denver hospital when a nineteen-year-old car crash victim was admitted to the intensive-care unit coughing up blood. The young man, a white supremacist skinhead sporting a swastika tattoo, was shocked to look up from his bed and see Kamau, a black man, taking care of him. The patient refused to have anything to do with his doctor. "He never talked to me directly; all of our dealings were via white nurses," Kamau writes. "They interpreted to him what I said, as if I spoke in another language. He never allowed his open eyes to rest on mine again."

Despite the difficulties, Kamau did his work and the patient recovered. The doctor had fulfilled the Hippocratic ideal to which he was sworn: being an honorable agent of the patient. Judging from the searching personal essay he wrote about the experience, I think Kamau would be deeply offended at the suggestion that a physician might compromise his standard of care for patients such as this hate-filled nineteen-year-old.

Claiming Bias

According to new conventional wisdom, however, it takes far less than an insufferably bigoted patient to cause a physician to lower his standard of treatment. A mismatch in race between doctor and patient—especially when the doctor is white and the patient is not—may be enough to trigger subtle, or not so subtle, biases that result in second-rate medical treatment and poorer health. "It is increasingly evident that African-Americans and other minority patients have strong grounds for doubting both the goodwill and the color blindness of White medical practitioners," writes Kenneth DeVille of the Department of Medical Humanities at the East Carolina University School of Medicine. No less authoritative a voice than the American Medical Association's official newspaper has claimed that "a growing body of research reports that racial disparities in health status can be explained, at least in part, by racism and discrimination within the health care system itself." This is why, according to the Reverend Al Sharpton, health will be the "new civil rights battlefront," a prediction echoed by other black leaders, including the Reverend Jesse Jackson, National Association for the Advancement of Colored People [NAACP] chairman Julian Bond and the Congressional Black Caucus.

In a 1998 radio address delivered during Black History Month, President Clinton spoke of race and health. "Nowhere are the divisions of race and ethnicity more sharply drawn than in the health of our people." It is indeed true that black Americans are less healthy than whites and Asians on a number of measures, such as life expectancy, infant mortality and death from cancer. This often remains true even when insurance coverage is taken into account. Beyond these facts, the president could only speculate when he said that perhaps one of the reasons for racial disparities is "discrimination in the delivery of health services."

Earlier Incidences of Bias

Given the history of systematic racial discrimination and segregation in the health care system, lingering bias seems, at first, plausible. Black patients were treated on separate and inferior hospital wards—a policy that persisted at many hospitals in the Deep South until the late 1960s. Once routinely barred from joining hospital staffs and medical societies, black physicians started their own institutions to treat other blacks who were denied adequate care by the white-controlled medical facilities. As late as the mid-1960s several medical schools had restrictions against admitting black students.

A particularly appalling episode in medical research was the Tuskegee Syphilis Study, whose purpose was to study the natural progression of the disease in black men. In the notorious "experiment," which lasted from 1932 to 1972, roughly four hundred black men in the late stages of syphilis were never told of their condition, never given any kind of treatment and never warned about transmitting it—grossly unethical practices that would never be tolerated today.

Decades later, however, accusations of medical bias still linger. According to Vanessa Northington Gamble, a physician and vice president of Community and Minority Programs at the Association of American Medical Colleges, "Tuskegee symbolizes for many African-Americans the racism that pervades American institutions, including the medical profession." In the fall of 1999 the U.S. Commission on Civil Rights informed Congress and the White House that "racism continue[s] to infect" the health care system. Earlier that year an official of the Association of American Medical Colleges commented on physicians' unwitting biases. "Most doctors think they are fair," he told the *Boston Globe*. "That they carry bias is very hard for them to think about."

Ignoring the Reasons for Health Disparities

For her part, Leslie Pickering Francis, a medical ethicist at the University of Utah, prefers to believe that "racism [is] the presumptive cause of . . . health care problems minorities face" until there is evidence to the contrary. This view is increasingly common—not too surprising considering the habit nowadays of presuming that discrimination inevitably lies beneath the surface of any race-related difference in social outcome. But evidence suggests that many race-related differences in health are not what they seem to observers like Professor Francis, Reverend Sharpton and the Commission on Civil Rights.

The charge of physician bias against minority patients is often made reflexively, overlooking the myriad complicated reasons for differences in care. In this [viewpoint] I present evidence that supports other interpretations of "health disparities," as they are often called. . . .

Differences in Health Problems

Less eye-catching than accusations of bias are the everyday aspects of clinical care that account for many of the recorded disparities. For example, one reason procedure rates differ is that medical problems do not necessarily occur with the same frequency across races. As a 1999 report from the Henry J. Kaiser Family Foundation points out, "It should be noted that every differential in care is not necessarily a problem and the level of care obtained by whites may not be the appropriate standard for comparison." Consider these facts: uterine fibroid tumors, and thus hysterectomies, are more common in black women than in whites, while osteoporosis-related fractures, and thus hip replacements, are rarer. Limb amputation is more common among black patients, typically because thicker atherosclerosis of the blood vessels in the leg makes it harder to perform limb-saving surgery.

Lowering Medical School Standards

[Kathryn Jean] Lopez: There's an interesting debate you highlight in your book in regard to racial preferences. What's the case for racial preferences in regard to enhancing minority health? How does that work? . . .

[Sally] Satel: The most striking aspect of racial preferences, in my view, is how far down into the applicant pool medical schools are reaching in order to have a diverse student body. In my chapter on race and health, I document the considerable differences in test scores and grades between incoming white and black (sometimes Hispanic) students and the trouble that the latter often have in medical school: higher dropout rates, multiple failures on boards.

We have lowered standards dramatically so that there will be more minority doctors. Of course, minority students who are admitted competitively do fine. It's just that, on average, grossly underprepared students perform poorly and, one reasonably fears, go on to become second-rate graduates.

Kathryn Jean Lopez and Sally Satel, *National Review Online*, January 13/14, 2001.

African Americans suffer stroke at many times the rate of whites yet undergo a procedure to unclog arteries in the neck (endarterectomy) only one-fourth as often. Racism? Unlikely. Some studies have documented a greater aversion to surgery and other invasive procedures among African American patients, but the more substantial reason, in the case of endarterectomy, is clinical. It turns out that whites tend to have their obstructions in the large, superficial carotid arteries of the neck region, which are readily accessible to surgery. Blacks, by comparison, tend to have their blockages in the branches of the carotids. These smaller vessels run deeper and further up into the head where the surgeon cannot reach them.

Thus, even without financial obstacles, an African American patient at high risk for stroke is far less likely than a white counterpart to undergo endarterectomy. Yet indoctrinologists like David R. Williams, a sociologist at the University of Michigan's Institute for Social Research, are quick to turn this disparity into evidence of bias. After all, they argue, if money is not an issue, then the difference in treatment *must* represent bias on the part of the doctors. *American Medical News*, the newspaper of the American Medical Association, gives voice to this view: "National studies, such as one that examined care at Dept. of Veterans Affairs medical facilities—where all of the patients have comparable insurance coverage—suggest 'racial disparities in the quality of medical care do not merely reflect the behavior of a few bad apples,' Dr. Williams said. 'The evidence is too overwhelming and the pattern is too pervasive.'"

Williams seems not to consider a different interpretation: the patients' clinical needs rather than the doctors' personal biases are dictating the care. Think about it: If not for concern about the patient (many of whom are treated in private hospitals and have health insurance), why wouldn't physicians perform a reimbursable procedure?

The Condition of Patients and Hospitals

Another consideration in performing procedures is the clinical condition of the patient. Does he have other medical problems that alter the risk-to-benefit ratio of a procedure and make the outcome less favorable? The treatment of heart disease, for example, often needs to be modified in the presence of uncontrolled high blood pressure and diabetes—conditions more typical of black patients with heart disease than of their white counterparts.

Then there is the site of care itself. Some hospitals simply do not offer certain cardiac procedures, such as bypass grafts or balloon angioplasty. Examining a sample taken from New York City hospitals, Dr. Lucian L. Leape of the Harvard School of Public Health and his colleagues found that about one-fifth of all patients needing these procedures do not get them, largely because those hospitals do not offer them. Leape found that failure to recommend these procedures—and hence to transfer a patient to a hospital where it could be performed—is equal across all groups of black, white and Hispanic patients. Conversely, when medical care is readily available for special patient populations (for example, the veterans' affairs medical centers or the military services), racial differences in treatment and outcome can melt away. For example, veterans with colorectal and prostate cancer show no race-related differences in treatment availability, treatment methods or survival rates. . . .

The racial disparities in health are real, but data do not point convincingly to systematic racial bias as a determinant.

"Experiencing harm as a result of receiving health care is a growing concern for the American public."

Medical Errors Are a Serious Problem

Quality Interagency Coordination Task Force

The Quality Interagency Coordination Task Force is a government organization established in 1998 to ensure that all the federal agencies that provide or regulate health care services work together to improve the quality of health care. In the following viewpoint, the task force contends that medical errors occur with alarming frequency. According to the authors, these errors are a result of poorly designed health care systems in which employees are overworked and mentally exhausted. The authors argue that mistakes in the administering of medications are the primary cause of patient death and harm.

As you read, consider the following questions:

1. In the authors' opinion, what must be the first priority of the health care industry?
2. Why does the task force believe that it is difficult to know how frequently medical errors occur?
3. According to the *Harvard Medical Practice Study*, cited by the authors, what percentage of injuries and deaths caused by drug reactions was preventable?

Excerpted from "Doing What Counts for Patient Safety: Federal Actions to Reduce Medical Errors and Their Impact," by Quality Interagency Coordination Task Force, February 2000.

The Institute of Medicine's (IOM's) release of *To Err Is Human* [in 1999] brought medical errors and patient safety the attention it has long needed but never had. The information presented in the report is not new. Indeed, many studies, some as early as the 1960s, showed that patients were frequently injured by the same medical care that was intended to help them. While evidence of medical error has existed for some time, the report succeeded in capturing the public's attention by revealing the magnitude of this pervasive problem and presenting it in a uniquely compelling fashion. The IOM estimates that medical errors cause between 44,000 and 98,000 deaths annually in the United States. Using the more conservative figure, medical errors rank as the eighth leading cause of death, killing more Americans than motor vehicle accidents, breast cancer, or AIDS. In addition to this extraordinary human toll, medical errors result in annual costs of $17 to $29 billion in the United States. Additionally, fear of becoming a victim of medical error may lead patients to delay obtaining potentially beneficial medical care, which may allow their illnesses to worsen.

Experiencing harm as a result of receiving health care is a growing concern for the American public. . . .

The Reasons Behind Medical Errors

The IOM report notes that the majority of medical errors today are not produced by negligence, lack of education, or lack of training. Rather, errors occur in our health care systems due to poor systems design and organizational factors, much as in any other industry. Health care workers are placed in systems and settings where errors are bound to happen. That is, the systems are designed to achieve a particular set of goals, but inadvertently produce a certain level of errors. For example, health care workers are sometimes expected to work 24-hour shifts to ensure patients are cared for and have some continuity of care, although it is known that overwork and fatigue lead to decreased mental concentration and alertness. These caregivers are expected to function in an environment that is not ergonomically designed for optimal work performance. They are expected to rely on their memories and deliver safe care without substantial investments in information technology or even the simple application of checklists. They often deliver care through a set of complex processes, although industry has shown that the probability of performing a task perfectly decreases as the number of steps in the process increases. Finally, they are expected to work in a climate where one error, even if not preventable, may mean a catastrophe or the end of a career. By not improving the systems in which medicine is practiced, the health care industry as a whole has not advocated a culture of safety and is not well organized to tackle the challenge of improving patient safety. Only when the entire industry is able to make patient safety and the reduction of medical errors its first priority will errors in medical practice be reduced.

The medical errors epidemic is a global problem. The United Kingdom, for example, has had some well-publicized difficulties with pediatric surgery outcomes in Bristol. British authorities estimate that 40,000 hospitalized patients die annually as a result of errors, which translates to a 3.7 percent overall rate of errors. The Australian Review of Professional Indemnity Arrangements for Health Care Professionals also found error to be a serious cause of morbidity and mortality. Australia, the United Kingdom, and Sweden are among the countries that have begun to address this issue. The British Ministry of Health is in the process of making funds available to researchers to investigate medical errors, and is reengineering its clinical governance programs to provide mechanisms to improve patient safety. Australia has included medical errors as part of its focus on quality, and is initiating a national system for error reduction with enhanced reporting mechanisms. However, efforts to actually translate the limited research available into practice are still at an early stage, at best. Approaches are likely to vary across nations because of differences in health care organization, attitudes toward regulation, and views on patient information and confidentiality. The evidence informing those approaches, however, is likely to be more universal. As a global leader, the United States has a responsibility to the many countries that do not have the resources to devote to the study of this issue.

Errors and other adverse events occur regularly in care settings, but the causes, frequency, severit ventability, and impact of these events on patient oi are not completely understood. A few studies have f alarmingly high prevalence of adverse events and medical errors in some hospitals. In two large studies of hospital admissions, one in New York using 1984 data and another in Colorado and Utah using 1992 data, the proportions of admissions in which there were adverse events (defined as injuries caused by medical management) were 2.9 and 3.7 percent, respectively. In the New York study, errors (defined as avoidable "mistakes in performance or thought") were determined to have caused more than half of the adverse events. However, the absence of standardized definitions of medical error, the lack of coordination and integration of systems to report and monitor errors, and the difficulty in distinguishing preventable errors from currently unavoidable adverse events hamper our understanding of this problem. It is unlikely that we can ever know the precise frequency with which errors occur in health care settings because we must rely on people to recognize that errors were made, to distinguish them from bad outcomes of appropriate treatment, and then to report them.

The Dangers of Pharmaceutical Drugs

Preventable injuries and deaths from pharmaceutical drugs are a growing problem that, according to some studies, represents a leading cause of death and patient harm in the United States. Although the methods used to measure the rate of errors associated with the use of drugs have significant limitations, researchers have estimated that more than 50 percent of prescriptions are used incorrectly. Problems related to the use of pharmaceutical drugs account for nearly 10 percent of all hospital admissions, and significantly contribute to increased morbidity and mortality in the United States.

In the *Harvard Medical Practice Study* of adverse medical events [published in 1991], which was based on 30,195 randomly selected records from 51 hospitals in New York State, the researchers found that drug complications represented 19 percent of all adverse events. The researchers concluded that ɔ8 percent of injuries and deaths due to drug reactions were preventable, and 27.6 percent of such complications were due to negligence. According to this study, antimicrobial drugs were the class of agents most commonly associated with adverse drug events. Misuse of antimicrobial drugs not only exposes individual patients to an increased risk of a poor treatment outcome, but also leads to the emergence and spread of drug-resistant microorganisms, which may place other patients and health care workers at risk of infection.

Markstein. © 1999 by Copley Media Services. Reprinted with permission.

The specific problem of medication errors has drawn considerable public attention, since all such errors are preventable. Medication errors—mistakes in writing prescriptions, dispensing or administering drugs—are a subset of the larger category of errors involving drugs. In a case-control study covering a 4-year period at a single hospital, it was determined that there was an almost 2-fold increase in the risk of death attributable to such errors. In the previously cited *Harvard Medical Practice Study*, 19.4 percent of all disabling adverse events were caused by drugs, of which 45 percent were due to medication errors. In that study, 30 percent of those with drug-related injuries died.

A Significant Health Concern

In addition to drug-related injuries and deaths that occur in hospitals, information is available indicating that preventable, drug-related injuries also occur at a high frequency among out-patients. In a study of 1,000 ambulatory patients drawn from a community, office-based medical practice, the researchers noted side effects from drugs in 42 patients (4.2 percent), including 23 who experienced preventable side effects. Well-understood drug-drug interactions are preventable, but there is evidence that physicians do not routinely screen for them, even when a patient's medication history is readily available. In a study of 424 randomly selected visits to a hospital emergency department, 47 percent of visits resulted in the patient receiving a prescription for a medication. In 10 percent of these instances, the new medication could potentially harm the patient due to an avoidable drug-drug interaction. In all of these cases, a medication history had been recorded and available to the prescribing physicians.

Thus, it can be seen that preventable and avoidable injuries due to drugs constitute a significant public health concern. The increasing use of drugs, the growing fragmentation of health care delivery, and the competing demands of an overburdened health care delivery system will, undoubtedly, accentuate these problems.

*"The medical care system, and particularly
doctors, are being scapegoated in pursuit of
others' political agendas."*

The Frequency of Medical Errors Has Been Exaggerated

David R. Zimmerman

In the following viewpoint, David R. Zimmerman claims
that reports on the dangers of medical errors are based on
exaggerated and out-of-date information. He contends that
the report issued by the Institute of Medicine (IOM)—the
chief source cited by those who exaggerate the frequency of
medical errors—was written without verification from independent sources and was therefore biased and unreliable.
According to Zimmerman, the political agenda of the IOM,
federal government, and media is to scapegoat medical practitioners while ignoring the need to improve health care systems. Zimmerman is the editor of *Probe*, a newsletter that
critiques science and the media, and an adjunct professor at
the Columbia Graduate School of Journalism.

As you read, consider the following questions:
1. What was former president Bill Clinton's response to the
   IOM report, as stated by Zimmerman?
2. On what basis does the author claim that the Harvard
   study was based on outdated information?
3. According to Zimmerman, what do Eric J. Thomas and
   Troyen A. Brennan believe is the likely cause of most
   medical errors?

S hocking!
     Between 44,000 and 100,0000 Americans die each year in hospitals as the result of medical errors.

Responses to the IOM Report

This devastating finding was announced [in late 1999] by the conservative Institute of Medicine (IOM), an arm of the similarly conservative—and recondite—National Academy of Sciences (NAS), in Washington, D.C. Congress and the President responded rapidly:

Senate hearings have already been held. Bills were introduced, and at least one has been passed and signed into law. President [Bill] Clinton's proposals and directives call for new federal and state offices to oversee patient safety, which, as the *New York Times* pointed out approvingly, "will now . . . be a federal and state responsibility," as well as a medical one. Tens, and eventually hundreds of millions of dollars will be committed to these efforts.

"President Clinton's proposals, or something similar, seem likely to become reality," health care reporter Robert Pear wrote in the *New York Times* (February 22, 2000), on page 1. One reason, he explained, is "the issue has great appeal to consumers, and this is an election year." [In fall 2000, Clinton called for the creation of a Center for Quality Improvement in Patient Safety. The Food and Drug Administration is also enhancing its role.]

In a word, pandering.

Much of the public debate is about finger-pointing: How to find ways to report medical errors to government officials. This concern was heightened by news coverage [in February 2000] of criminal charges against a New York City obstetrician, Allan Zarkin, M.D., who—bizarrely—had carved his initials into the belly of a woman whose baby he had just delivered. The IOM report, entitled *To Err Is Human*, and its dire findings, thus have become a persisting source of public concern and policy debate. Surely, the data to back this indictment of America's health care system must be rock solid!

Problem: They're not.

Not at all!

This, too, suggests that politics, rather than scientific understanding, is driving the headline scramble. It also raises our sense that, as has happened before, the medical care system, and particularly doctors, are being scapegoated in pursuit of others' political agendas.

Let's look at the evidence behind the IOM report, which was written by a committee chaired by business administration expert William C. Richardson, Ph.D., president and CEO of the W.R. Kellogg Foundation, in Battle Creek, Michigan. The report is 221 pages long, and contains hundreds of footnotes. In fact, however, the report's scary findings are based on just two studies.

A More Positive Approach

The [health care] maxim ["First, do no harm"] reinforces the often dysfunctional concept of fault. After all, if we promise to do no harm, when harm inevitably does occur, someone must be to blame. This blaming mentality reinforces the syndrome of denial. Moreover, the [medical] profession becomes unwitting coconspirators with the reviled tort system, which is founded on the concept of finding fault. Rather than fault finding, we need a more evenhanded approach to recognize and acknowledge risks (along with benefits), unforeseen harms, and human error. We need to maintain accountability. But we need a more positive approach that rewards efforts to identify and address errors and otherwise reduce harm.

James D. Shelton, *Journal of the American Medical Association*, December 6, 2000.

Here's what the report says, on page 1:

Two large studies, one conducted in Colorado and Utah and the other in New York, found that adverse events occurred in 2.9% and 3.7% of hospitalizations, respectively. In Colorado and Utah hospitals, 8.8% of adverse events led to death, as compared to 13.6% in New York hospitals. In both these studies, over half of these adverse events resulted from medical errors and could have been prevented.

Extrapolating these estimates to all U.S. hospital admissions, the IOM panel says, this comes to 44,000 deaths annually (based on Colorado and Utah), or "as high as 98,000 deaths," based on the New York study.

The New York data, from what is called the *Harvard*

Medical Practice Study, come from two Harvard physicians, Lucian L. Leape, M.D., and Troyen A. Brennan, M.D. (who also is a public health specialist and a lawyer), and several associates. It was published in the *New England Journal of Medicine (NEJM)* in 1991—February 7 of that year, to be precise. But this was not fresh information even back then. The hospital records upon which the Harvard study was based came from 1984.

The findings provoked little controversy when they were published. Only two letters to the editor about the reports appeared in the *NEJM* in the next six months. Neither breathed fire.

Leape and Brennan subsequently raised their estimate of "iatrogenic injury" to 180,000 deaths per annum. Leape was also a member of the IOM panel.

No Independent Sources

The Colorado-Utah study is more recent, and might be expected to add confirmatory evidence from another source. Two problems: The key part of it had not been published when the IOM report came out. So it has not been available while the intense debate on medical error rolls onward. What is more, the IOM report fails to reveal this important fact: The Colorado-Utah study was conducted by the same researchers as the one in New York. Brennan, a senior author of the New York report, is also an author of the Colorado-Utah report, as is the Harvard statistician Joseph P. Newhouse, Ph.D. Journalists must get two independent sources for major stories. Should the Institute of Medicine settle for less?

The IOM report has two references from the Colorado-Utah study. One is in a journal called *Inquiry*, published by the regional Blue Cross and Blue Shield in Rochester, N.Y. Brennan is on the editorial board. *Inquiry's* circulation is 2500. In thirty years of medical reporting, we'd never heard of it. We doubt that many doctors, reporters or public health pundits have either.

The published *Inquiry* paper, however, is on the fiscal "costs of medical injuries." It does not discuss the scary morbidity and mortality findings, or the extrapolation to 44,000 annual deaths in the U.S. that are purportedly based on them.

This information is cited in the IOM report as "forth-coming in March [2000]" in a second publication, identified as *Medical Care*. This journal is similarly obscure. It took us ten days and thirty phone calls to find it in time to cover it here. It was published on February 28, 2000—long after everybody in Washington had made up his or her mind about it, based on the IOM report summary and news accounts.

There is this additional problem: The Colorado-Utah data also are stale. They were collected in 1992, and hence are eight years old!

Contradictory Recommendations

The first author is ex-Harvard internist Eric J. Thomas, M.D., who is now in Houston. Brennan, again, is a co-author, and the study is a replay of the one in New York. But: significantly lower levels of disability and death were found in Colorado and Utah hospitals. The authors do not use the phrases "medical error" or "medical mistake" in their discussion. They report only adverse events and negligent ones. Their last words, unavailable to the public 'til now, should give pause. While much of the public debate has focused on whether and how to report individual health care providers' errors and mistakes, Thomas and his colleagues say that "many errors in medicine are likely the result of system failures rather than just one practitioner committing an error." Improving health care systems thus might offer "exciting opportunities to improve patient safety."

In other words, the investigators upon whom the IOM committee based their recommendations end up with a proposal that is diametrically opposed to the finger-pointing that the IOM report, the President, Congress, and the press have indulged in.

Has the public been served by this policy debate?

Periodical Bibliography

The following articles have been selected to supplement the diverse views presented in this chapter.

Lawrence K. Altman	"The Wrong Foot, and Other Tales of Surgical Error," *New York Times*, December 11, 2001.
Susan Brink	"HMOs Were the Right Rx," *U.S. News & World Report*, March 9, 1998.
Stephen Chapman	"The Many Wrongs Of . . ." *Conservative Chronicle*, October 20, 1999.
Consumers' Research Magazine	"Medical Errors: Time to Take Action," January 2000.
Amy Goldstein	"Who Lacks Health Insurance?" *Washington Post National Weekly Edition*, October 11, 1999.
Scott Hensley	"Talking About HMOs," *Wall Street Journal*, February 21, 2001.
Robert Kuttner	"Incremental Reform Toward What?" *American Prospect*, February 14, 2000.
Jennifer M. Mellor and Jeffrey Milyo	"Reexaming the Evidence of an Ecological Association Between Income Inequality and Health," *Journal of Health, Politics, Policy and Law*, June 2001.
Donald L. Price	"A Better Health-Care System," *World & I*, April 1999.
Helen Redmond	"The Crisis in Health Care," *International Socialist Review*, Summer 1999.
Alejandro Reuss	"Cause of Death: Inequality," *Dollars and Sense*, May/June 2001.
Sally Satel	"Sick Sisters: How Feminist Politics Is Warping Medicine," *American Enterprise*, April/May 2001.
James D. Shelton	"The Harm of 'First, Do No Harm,'" *Journal of the American Medical Association*, December 6, 2000.
Barbara Starfield	"Is U.S. Health Really the Best in the World?" *Journal of the American Medical Association*, July 26, 2000.
Diana Wiley	"Mistakes That Kill," *Maclean's*, August 13, 2001.

CHAPTER 2

Is Alternative
Medicine Effective?

Chapter Preface

The term "alternative medicine" is something of a misnomer. It suggests that such treatments developed as a response to methods commonly used by contemporary Western doctors. In fact, some "alternative" treatments predate modern Western medicine by hundreds, or even thousands, of years. One example is herbal medicine, which is used as a primary method of treatment by approximately 80 percent of the world.

In his book *Understanding Alternative Medicine: New Health Paths in America*, Lawrence Tyler writes, "The argument can be made that there is more hard evidence for the longevity of herbal medicine than for any other medical technique." Five-thousand-year-old Sumerian clay tablets refer to the use of herbs. Other historical documentation concerning the longevity of herbal medicine includes the Chinese work *Pen T'Shao Kang Mu*, written circa 2500 B.C., and a 3,500-year-old Egyptian papyrus. Herbal medicine was also used among the ancient Hindus, Greeks, and Romans. In modern society, two of the most common types of herbal medicine are Chinese and ayurvedic.

Chinese practitioners use herbal formulas to ensure a balance between the forces known as "yin" and "yang." Ginseng is one of the best known of these herbs; its uses include treating arthritis and increasing endurance. Other popular herbs are cloves, which treat abdominal pain and lack of appetite, and Chinese licorice, a common remedy for tonifying, or strengthening, the spleen (considered a remedy for poor appetite and diarrhea) and moistening the lung, which relieves coughing.

Ayurvedic medicine, which developed in India, uses herbs to help balance the "three humors" of the human body. Those humors are air, water, and fire; each corresponds to different body parts and ailments. For example, the fire humor is associated with the small intestine, the stomach, and digestive problems. Herbs and plants used to treat ailments associated with the fire humor include cascara bark, sarsaparilla, and dandelion root. Other popular cures in ayurvedic medicine are bala, which is used to treat heart disease and arthritis, and guduchi, which is believed to purify the blood and help heal eye disorders.

Despite the worldwide popularity and long history of herbal medicine, many people in the modern medical community question its safety and efficacy. In the following chapter, the authors debate whether herbs and other alternative treatments can adequately treat health problems.

VIEWPOINT

1

> "*Scientific allopathic medicine can incorporate hundreds of herbal therapies without compromising scientific standards.*"

Herbal Medicine Can Be Safe and Effective

Lawrence Tyler

In the following viewpoint, Lawrence Tyler asserts that herbal remedies can effectively treat illnesses provided that the dosage and quality of the herbs are standardized. He argues that the United States should follow Germany's lead in the regulation of proven herbal medications such as ginkgo biloba and St. John's wort. Tyler concludes that the U.S. government and the pharmaceutical industry need to coordinate an effort to properly study herbal medicine. Tyler is a professor of sociology at Western Michigan University in Kalamazoo and the author of *Understanding Alternative Medicine: New Health Paths in America*, from which this excerpt was taken.

As you read, consider the following questions:

1. According to Tyler, what is the "romantic perspective" of many herbalists?
2. What is the most frequently prescribed herbal medication in Germany, according to the author?
3. In Tyler's view, which government organizations need to cooperate in order to examine phytotherapy?

Excerpted from *Understanding Alternative Medicine: New Health Paths in America*, by Lawrence Tyler (Binghamton, NY: Haworth Herbal Press, 2000). Copyright © 2000 by the Haworth Press, Inc. Reprinted with permission.

In the past, but also continuing today, many different schools of herbalists have operated from a romantic perspective that the healing power of herbal treatment derives from a spiritual-holistic base, that some ritual process is crucial to the healing, and that some special esoteric knowledge or communion with nature is at the source of wellness. These vestiges of a shamanistic perspective, regardless of their efficacy, are a major barrier preventing large-scale incorporation of herbal medicines into scientific, mainstream medical practice.

Questioning Herbal Treatments

The placebo power of ritual and emotional support, at which many traditional herbalists excel, [has been] discussed in terms of its healing utility. But for the moment, putting aside these real and valuable elements of treatment, some pragmatic questions remain: (1) Do traditional herbalists really know the epidemiology of what they are treating? (2) Are their prescriptive skills based on a sure knowledge of the plant materials they use? (3) Will the crude plant materials used by traditional herbalists yield the qualitative and quantitative dosage of active ingredient that will ameliorate the medical problem?

The first two questions are endlessly controversial, and have been debated for decades by the opposing camps. There is a point at which pursuing these tradition-versus-science issues is counter-productive. However, the third question is now more likely to yield an answer based on evidence rather than opinion. The focus on this question is part of the development of what some experts have called "rational phytotherapy." Rational phytotherapy's distinctive feature is the standardization of herb- and plant-based medicines. It has developed from the realization that herbs can have medical efficacy, but only through the standardization of qualitative and quantitative dosage. [According to Volker Schulz, Rudolf Hänsel, and Varro E. Tyler:]

> Herbs are natural products. Nature does not supply its products with a consistent, standardized composition . . . the constituents of medical herbs can vary greatly as a result of genetic factors, climate, soil quality, and other external factors.

The material derived from cultivated medicinal plants shows smaller variations than material gathered from the wild. . . . Thus, standardization of the extract begins with selection and mixing of the herbal raw materials.

If nothing else, this should at least lay to rest the issue of wild versus cultivated herbs. Cultivated herbs are a more reliable source of medicine than those found in the wild.

The Future of Phytotherapy

Following the pattern of the use and acceptance of rational phytotherapy in Europe, and especially Germany, the future of herbal medicine will more closely resemble the modern pharmaceutical industry than the village herbalist. [According to Schulz, Hänsel, and Tyler:]

Phytomedicines are medicinal plants that contain plant materials as their pharmacologically active component. . . . For most phytomedicines, the specific ingredients that determine the pharmacologic activity are unknown. The crude drug (dried herb) or a whole extract derived from it is considered to be the active ingredient.

The key word distinguishing phytotherapy from traditional herbalism is "extracts," which "are concentrated preparations of a liquid, powdered, or viscous consistency that are ordinarily made from dried plant parts (the crude drug) by maceration or percolation. . . . Two key factors determine the internal composition of an extract: the quality of the herbal raw material and the production process."

Even laboratory-produced plant extracts are sometimes of dubious quality due to the raw materials used. Commercial producers operate in a marketplace where brokers and suppliers offer surplus and ungraded raw materials at cut-rate prices. . . .

Advocates of phytotherapy point to Germany as having the most enlightened standards, controls, and legislation [Schulz, Hänsel, and Tyler write]:

In Germany, the use of plant drugs is a science . . . the principal reason is, without question, the enlightened system of laws and regulations governing the sale and use of such products in that country.

Basically, the regulations in Germany permit phytomedicines to be sold either as self-selected or prescription drugs provided there is absolute proof of their safety and reasonable certainty of the efficacy. The words "reasonable certainty" are extremely important here. They require that some scientific and clinical evidence be provided prior to approval, but the requirements are not the same as would be necessary for a new chemical entity. Because patent protection it [*sic*] not ordinarily available for these ancient drugs, pharmaceutical companies are generally unwilling to invest the hundreds of millions of dollars required to prove them effective by the same standards applied to totally new synthetic drugs. They are, however, willing to invest more modest amounts in the scientific and clinical testing needed to establish reasonable certainty of efficacy.

Alternative Medicine Standards in Germany

That has been and continues to be done in Germany. Data regarding safety and efficacy submitted to a specific body designated Commission E of the German Federal Health Agency (now the Federal Institute for Drugs and Medical Devices) have resulted in judgments validating the utility of several hundred different phytomedicines. The most frequently approved phytotherapies in Germany are those classified as single-herb products [according to Schulz, Hänsel, and Tyler]:

> In 1995, phytomedicines accounted for approximately 7 percent of all prescription medications covered by public health insurance in Germany, with total sales of about 2 billion DM. Two-thirds of the prescriptions were for single-herb products, i.e., products whose active ingredients derive from only one medicinal plant. Just 5 herbs account for approximately 60 percent of these prescriptions, and 28 herbs account for more than 90 percent.

Among the most commonly prescribed herbal medications in Germany, the best selling single-herb product is ginkgo biloba, followed by St. John's wort. Ginkgo biloba has been used in traditional Chinese medicine (TCM) for centuries. Today its primary TCM use is in treating asthma. Western research has placed ginkgo extract among "the class of nootropic drugs, i.e., agents that act on the central nervous system and tend to improve cognitive performance" [write Schulz, Hänsel, and Tyler].

China and other east Asian areas, as well as France and the United States, continue to be the primary sources of the bulk plant materials. The leaves of the plant yield the desired extract, high in flavonoid glycosides. The extract content is influenced by the time of harvest and condition of tree, as well as soil and climate.

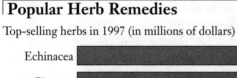

Popular Herb Remedies

Top-selling herbs in 1997 (in millions of dollars)

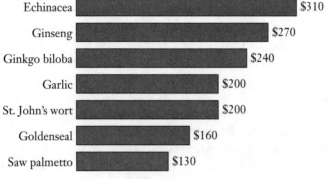

Echinacea $310
Ginseng $270
Ginkgo biloba $240
Garlic $200
St. John's wort $200
Goldenseal $160
Saw palmetto $130

Food and Drug Administration, *Journal of the American Medical Association, Nutrition Business Journal.*

In Germany, only the extracts (not the leaves themselves) meeting strict standards can be used in herbal medicines for human use. The standardized extraction "process eliminates unwanted components, including those that make the product less stable or pose an excessive toxocologic risk—fats, waxes, tannins, proanthocyanidins, biflavonoids, ginkgol, ginkgolic acids, proteins, and mineral components. The extracts suitable for use in drug manufacture are designated in the technical literature as EGb 761 and LI 1370."

A substantial body of research literature on the pharmacologic efficacy of ginkgo biloba extract–based drugs has been published in Germany, meeting the standards of the German government. [Schulz, Hänsel, and Tyler write:] "The *Rote Liste 1995* (Red List—the German equivalent of *Physician's Desk Reference*) contains a total of eight allopathic ginkgo preparations, five of which meet the specifications of the 1994 Commission E monograph (extracts EGb 761 and LI 1370); the three others do not."

St. John's wort and all other single-herb phytotherapies, are held to the same high standard in Germany. St. John's wort (*Hypericum perforatum*) has been used for centuries in Europe and Asia for mood disorders. As an herbal antidepressant, it is now one of the most widely used herbal medicines in the world (which may also say something about the current mood in the world). The plant grows throughout Europe, Asia, and North and South America. Solid clinical evidence confirms the efficacy of St. John's wort extract-based preparations "in the treatment of depression or at least certain of its symptoms. . . . The *Rote Liste 1995* identifies 18 single-herb hypericum products that are marketed in Germany" [according to Schulz, Hänsel, and Tyler].

The distinction between rational phytotherapies (plant-based drugs for which safety has been scientifically documented) and other herbal remedies has increased the medical choices of German consumers and given them a prescription option that is usually less costly than conventional drugs. German drug law has laid the basis for this expansion of choices. [Schulz, Hänsel, and Tyler write:]

> The fifth amendment of the German Drug Law of August 9, 1994, laid the groundwork for drawing a distinction between rational and irrational plant medicines. This amendment states that scientifically proven phytomedicines (most likely single-herb products) will be evaluated for pharmaceutical quality, efficacy, and safety in a normal approval process and will be given a corresponding approval number that physicians can recognize.

Learning from Germany

This German experience seems to be an excellent example of how scientific allopathic medicine can incorporate hundreds of herbal therapies without compromising scientific standards. The relevant question is whether this path could be taken in the United States. If, as the *Journal of the American Medical Association* (*JAMA*) editor stated in the November 11, 1998 issue, the American Medical Association (AMA) goal is to halt the "uncritical acceptance of untested and unproven alternative medical therapies," then emulating the German example of the promotion of rational phytotherapy would seem to be a very good starting point.

The research base is available. If the AMA does not choose to accept the existing studies, then, as with all real science, these studies can be replicated. Any such solution, in reality, would have to be implemented through the coordinated effort of the Food and Drug Administration (FDA), National Institutes of Health (NIH), AMA, and the pharmaceutical industry. This medical-industrial complex of government regulation, research efforts, professional standards, and industrial wealth is the power base from which all medical change in America is instigated. For the time being, at least, the AMA is showing signs of wanting to respond to the growing use of alternative medicine in America. Their stated concern is the indiscriminate nature of this use. Urging the FDA and pharmaceutical companies to examine rational phytotherapy would be an excellent first step toward minimizing the nonrational medical decisions now being made by so many patients.

| *"The wonderful herbs and supplements that are supposed to help without side effects aren't quite so harmless."*

Herbal Medicine Is Dangerous

David Bloomberg

Herbal remedies can lead to dangerous and sometimes fatal side effects, David Bloomberg asserts in the following viewpoint. According to Bloomberg, these side effects include kidney failure, strokes, seizures, and high blood pressure. He maintains that herbal medicines should be tested thoroughly to ensure that they are safe and effective. Bloomberg is chairman and cofounder of The Rational Examination Association of Lincoln Land (REALL), a nonprofit educational and scientific organization in Illinois.

As you read, consider the following questions:
1. As stated by Bloomberg, what are some of the dangerous side effects of comfrey?
2. According to Bloomberg, why are some potential herb-drug interaction problems unknown?
3. What does the author find interesting about St. John's wort's effect on pregnancy and fertility?

[S ince 1999] there has been an increased focus on reports indicating that dietary supplements, which are supposed to help you, may actually cause all sorts of problems. These problems range from contaminants in the supplements to dangers from the untested herbs and harmful interactions with important medications.

It seems that almost every week, there's another study that shows how the wonderful herbs and supplements that are supposed to help without side effects aren't quite so harmless. This [viewpoint] is by no means comprehensive, but attempts to chronicle some of the reported problems that have come up when using virtually unregulated herbs and supplements.

Contamination and Dangers

As an example of the contamination problem, Reuters reported (1/20/00) that high levels of polychlorinated biphenyls (PCBs) were found in five different brands of shark liver oil capsules. PCBs are potential carcinogens, so it is rather ironic that the shark liver oil is sold to supposedly help fight cancer, among other things.

In addition, some other supplements are contaminated with steroids, digitalis, or heavy metals like lead and arsenic. It was reported that some supposedly herbal supplements actually contain animal parts. Besides the problems this may cause for vegetarians, it also poses potential health risks, because we don't know where those animal parts really came from or how they were reprocessed.

A March 2000 Associated Press article discussed the dangers of comfrey, which is supposedly anti-inflammatory and antibacterial. It is widely available here in the U.S., but restricted in Germany and Canada. One doctor noted that not only are the claims made for it unproven, but there is evidence that it can "destroy small veins in the liver and can result in abdominal pain, liver enlargement and liver failure." In other words, it is hazardous to consume even without contamination.

MSNBC reported in March 2000 that poison control centers across the country have been reporting potentially dangerous adverse reactions to ginseng, St. John's wort,

63

ephedra, melatonin, and others. In one particularly heinous case, a woman gave her 18-month-old child eucalyptus oil because a store clerk told her it was good for fever. The child ended up suffering permanent neurological damage and almost died.

MSNBC also reported, in October 2000, that an herbal mixture that is supposed to fight prostate cancer, "PC-SPES," has a host of side effects including potentially fatal blood clots in up to 5% of those who use it!

In November 2000, they reported on a particularly scary trend: People with allergies are taking supplements without realizing they may be making those allergies worse! Indeed, echinacea is closely related to ragweed, and, [earlier in 2001], researchers reported 24 cases of the herb causing asthma attacks, hives, and anaphylactic reactions. One doctor noted, "Some of these people have inhalant allergies to grasses and weeds yet they're taking herbal substances—that doesn't make sense." She went on: "Many people take alternative medicines because they think they're safe and natural but people with allergies or allergic asthma could be potentially made worse."

Several news agencies reported in June 2000 on a Chinese herb, Aristolochia fangchi, that is supposed to help weight loss, but actually is linked to kidney failure and now urinary tract cancer. In addition to being sold straight, this herb sometimes appears, almost like a contaminant, in other supplements. This one is bad enough that the Food and Drug Administration (FDA) can act, because the supplement has been proven dangerous. They have banned import of the herb.

Another herb taken for weight loss, ephedra (also known as ma huang) has been the focus of a battle between the FDA and supplement manufacturers for over three years. The manufacturers had criticized the FDA for their testing methods, so the FDA went to independent investigators. Those investigators found that, if anything, ephedra may be more dangerous than originally thought! They were planning to release their results in a journal article in December [2000], but felt their findings important enough to make them public a month early, instead. Their study found numerous cases of strokes, heart attacks, and other serious side effects linked to ephedra—up to and including death.

Dangerous Interactions

More important than these issues are the drug interaction issues. Below are some of the problems that have been encountered and reported recently. Because Congress will not let the FDA regulate such "supplements," it's unknown how many more potential interaction problems there might be.

The Associated Press reported (2/11/00) that St. John's wort can interfere with drugs used by HIV-positive patients and those with heart transplants. This information comes from two different studies published in the medical journal, the *Lancet*. In the study on heart transplant patients, those who took St. John's wort actually started to reject their new hearts! Both of these are important because St. John's wort is taken to supposedly combat depression, and both of these groups are likely to suffer depression, thus making it more likely they could take the supplement in combination with their drugs.

In more recent news, Reuters Health reported (10/16/00) on two patients who suffered rejection of their transplanted kidneys because of St. John's wort. One had to undergo a second transplant because of the herb. *Discover* magazine discussed Adriane Fugh-Berman, a doctor at George Washington University School of Medicine who has been looking at herb/drug interactions. She has noted that St. John's wort can cause confusion, nausea, and diarrhea when taken with Prozac or other antidepressants. In March 2000, anesthesiologists noted that St. John's wort may affect the way people wake up out of anesthesia.

In May 2000, MSNBC reported on a study showing that St. John's wort may also weaken the effectiveness of birth control pills.

An August 2000 article on Health Central noted that St. John's wort and other herbs may interfere with fertility (in both men and women). This raises the interesting point that it may interfere both if you're trying to get pregnant and if you're trying to avoid it!

A January 2001, article notes that the American Academy of

Opthalmology warns that St. John's wort can make your eyes more susceptible to UV light, which increases cataract risk.

The Effects of Vitamin C

The ever-popular vitamin C has often been recommended in megadoses by supplement proponents. Even if it doesn't help much, they said, it won't hurt. Well, it turns out that might not be true. In March 2000, Associated Press had an article discussing research that indicates megadoses of vitamin C may speed up clogging of the arteries. Clogged arteries, of course, can lead to heart attacks and strokes. Ironically, some have promoted vitamin C megadoses as a way to protect against problems with the circulatory system.

Natural Herbs Are Not Superior

Paraherbalists claim that products made by the metabolic processes of plants or animals possess an innate superiority over identical products synthesized in a chemical laboratory. The falsity of this claim was demonstrated as far back as 1828 when the German chemist Friedrich Wohler synthesized urea from inorganic materials. Wohler's synthetic urea was identical in every respect with the urea biosynthesized and excreted by animals or biosynthesized and accumulated by many species of higher fungi. Thus, statements like, "The pharmaceutical industry needs to stop fooling around with dangerous synthetic chemicals and return, once again, to the more natural substances God has placed upon this earth for our health and benefit," are derived from baseless belief rather than scientific methodology.

Varro E. Tyler, "False Tenets of Paraherbalism," www.quackwatch.com.

Later that same month, many news outlets reported that vitamin C had also been implicated as possibly making cancer worse! While solid results aren't in yet, it appears that megadoses of vitamin C may protect tumors from radiation and chemotherapy. It has been found that cancer cells contain large amounts of the vitamin, which seems to protect those cells from damage.

In August 2000, a report in the journal *Archives of Biochemistry and Biophysics* discussed a study that showed, contrary to accepted wisdom, that vitamin C neutralizes chemicals that contribute to aging and various diseases; in smokers it may actually be the other way around. The research found that in the presence of cigarette smoke and saliva, vitamin C actually "became a harmful oxidizing substance," according to Dr. Abraham Reznick, the lead researcher.

And to further pile on, an April 2000 report issued by the Institute of Medicine said there is no evidence that large doses of vitamins C and E (and other antioxidants) prevent chronic diseases. Indeed, for the first time ever, they set upper limits on how much of these a person should take due to toxicity concerns (such as those discussed above) and noted that most people get enough nutrients from the foods they eat and don't need to take these vitamin supplements at all.

So much for the "it can't hurt" philosophy.

Further Dangers of Herbal Supplements

A new French study found that people taking ispaghula husk—a fiber supplement that is supposed to prevent colon cancer—actually have a higher risk of getting pre-cancerous polyps. This effect is worsened when they take it with calcium, which is also supposed to prevent colon cancer!

Black cohosh may cause the blood vessels of the eye to clot, change the cornea's curvature, and make contact lenses intolerable.

Ginseng may enhance estrogen levels and interfere with the anti-cancer drug tamoxifen. It may also disrupt the effectiveness of glaucoma and blood pressure medication.

Echinacea may react with chemotherapy drugs.

Discover magazine reports that ginkgo biloba can cause bleeding when taken with warfarin, an anti-clotting drug. The American Academy of Opthalmology notes that it also might cause bleeding in the eye.

Yohimbine can cause high blood pressure when used with some antidepressants.

Still more interactions were listed in May 2000 by *U.S. News & World Report*. Among the drug interactions listed were:

Licorice (the herb, not the candy) is supposed to help upset stomach and ulcers, but can interact with heart and blood pressure medications and make it more difficult for the heart to contract.

Ma huang is used as a stimulant, but may reduce the effectiveness of blood pressure medications.

Mate and Guarana are herbs that are supposed to help weight loss, but may slow the body's ability to get rid of clozapine, a drug used to treat schizophrenia. If taken together, the clozapine may build up in the body and kill bone marrow.

Shankapulshpi is supposed to treat epileptic seizures, but has the ironic effect of reducing the levels of anti-seizure medicine Dilantin, which could lead to more seizures.

In addition to the problems with St. John's wort, CNN and Business Wire both reported in March [2001] that anesthesiologists and nurse anesthetists are concerned about patients' use of many other herbs. Some anesthesiologists have noted problems with blood pressure, poor clotting, and excessive bleeding in patients who have taken ginseng, ginkgo biloba, ginger, ephedra, and other herbs.

Supplements and Pregnancy

On December 12, 2000, the medical director for the March of Dimes held a press conference to warn pregnant women, and those women who may become pregnant, about the use of herbal and other supplements. Because so many of these have not faced any real scientific testing with regard to their safety, he noted, "pregnant women who think they are doing everything right to ensure the health of their baby may unknowingly be causing harm."

He further explained that the assumption of a product being safe just because it's natural is simply false.

An article on MSNBC (12/12/00) gave several examples of dangerous herbs: Blue cohosh may cause fetal heart defects.

Hellebore, which is supposed to reduce cramps and morning sickness, may cause miscarriage or cleft palate.

Hemlock causes cleft palate and clubfeet.

Tragacanth (a laxative) can cause miscarriage or clubfeet.

These were just a few examples out of many potentially dangerous supplements.

How many more of these reports need to come out before somebody realizes it's time to do something about it? Even if these supplements were to somehow live up to the claims people make for them (which is rather doubtful), they still need to be tested for side effects and interactions. The defense that a substance is "natural" and therefore implied to be safe doesn't hold up in the face of an ever-increasing amount of evidence to the contrary. Maybe some herbs and supplements work; maybe not. But all need to be examined for both safety and effectiveness.

*"Acupuncture may be a reasonable option
for a number of clinical conditions."*

Acupuncture Is a Useful Treatment

National Institutes of Health

Acupuncture is a promising treatment for many medical conditions such as nausea, lower back pain, and addiction, the National Institutes of Health (NIH) maintains in the following viewpoint. In addition, the NIH argues that acupuncture has fewer adverse side effects compared to commonly used Western medical treatments. The NIH asserts that further research is needed to understand how acupuncture works and how its use in conventional medicine can be expanded. The NIH, which is part of the U.S. Department of Health and Human Services, works to improve universal human health.

As you read, consider the following questions:
1. What is the paradox of acupuncture research, according to the National Institutes of Health?
2. According to the World Health Organization, how many conditions have been treated with acupuncture?
3. In the opinion of the National Institutes of Health, what issues should be clarified before acupuncture is readily available?

Excerpted from "Acupuncture," National Institutes of Health consensus statement, November 3–5, 1997.

1. What Is the Efficacy of Acupuncture?

Acupuncture is a complex intervention that may vary for different patients with similar chief complaints. The number and length of treatments and the specific points used may vary among individuals and during the course of treatment. Given this reality, it is perhaps encouraging that there exist a number of studies of sufficient quality to assess the efficacy of acupuncture for certain conditions.

According to contemporary research standards, there is a paucity of high-quality research assessing efficacy of acupuncture compared with placebo or sham acupuncture. The vast majority of papers studying acupuncture in the biomedical literature consist of case reports, case series, or intervention studies with designs inadequate to assess efficacy. . . .

Responding to Acupuncture

As with other types of interventions, some individuals are poor responders to specific acupuncture protocols. Both animal and human laboratory and clinical experience suggest that the majority of subjects respond to acupuncture, with a minority not responding. Some of the clinical research outcomes, however, suggest that a larger percentage may not respond. The reason for this paradox is unclear and may reflect the current state of the research.

There is clear evidence that needle acupuncture is efficacious for adult postoperative and chemotherapy nausea and vomiting and probably for the nausea of pregnancy.

Much of the research is on various pain problems. There is evidence of efficacy for postoperative dental pain. There are reasonable studies (although sometimes only single studies) showing relief of pain with acupuncture on diverse pain conditions such as menstrual cramps, tennis elbow, and fibromyalgia. This suggests that acupuncture may have a more general effect on pain. However, there are also studies that do not find efficacy for acupuncture in pain.

There is evidence that acupuncture does not demonstrate efficacy for cessation of smoking and may not be efficacious for some other conditions.

Although many other conditions have received some attention in the literature and, in fact, the research suggests some exciting potential areas for the use of acupuncture, the quality or quantity of the research evidence is not sufficient to provide firm evidence of efficacy at this time. . . .

Treatable Conditions

2. What Is the Place of Acupuncture in the Treatment of Various Conditions for Which Sufficient Data Are Available, in Comparison or in Combination With Other Interventions (Including No Intervention)?

Assessing the usefulness of a medical intervention in practice differs from assessing formal efficacy. In conventional practice, clinicians make decisions based on the characteristics of the patient, clinical experience, potential for harm, and information from colleagues and the medical literature. In addition, when more than one treatment is possible, the clinician may make the choice taking into account the patient's preferences. While it is often thought that there is substantial research evidence to support conventional medical practices, this is frequently not the case. This does not mean that these treatments are ineffective. The data in support of acupuncture are as strong as those for many accepted Western medical therapies.

One of the advantages of acupuncture is that the incidence of adverse effects is substantially lower than that of many drugs or other accepted medical procedures used for the same conditions. As an example, musculoskeletal conditions, such as fibromyalgia, myofascial pain, and tennis elbow, or epicondylitis, are conditions for which acupuncture may be beneficial. These painful conditions are often treated with, among other things, anti-inflammatory medications (aspirin, ibuprofen, etc.) or with steroid injections. Both medical interventions have a potential for deleterious side effects but are still widely used and are considered acceptable treatments. The evidence supporting these therapies is no better than that for acupuncture.

In addition, ample clinical experience, supported by some research data, suggests that acupuncture may be a reasonable option for a number of clinical conditions. Examples are postoperative pain and myofascial and low back pain. Examples of disorders for which the research evidence is less convincing but for which there are some positive clinical trials include addiction, stroke rehabilitation, carpal tunnel syndrome, osteoarthritis, and headache. Acupuncture treatment for many conditions such as asthma or addiction should be part of a comprehensive management program.

Many other conditions have been treated by acupuncture; the World Health Organization, for example, has listed more than 40 for which the technique may be indicated.

How Acupuncture Works

3. What Is Known About the Biological Effects of Acupuncture That Helps Us Understand How It Works?

Many studies in animals and humans have demonstrated that acupuncture can cause multiple biological responses. These responses can occur locally, i.e., at or close to the site of application, or at a distance, mediated mainly by sensory neurons to many structures within the central nervous system. This can lead to activation of pathways affecting various physiological systems in the brain as well as in the periphery.

A focus of attention has been the role of endogenous opioids in acupuncture analgesia. Considerable evidence supports the claim that opioid peptides are released during acupuncture and that the analgesic effects of acupuncture are at least partially explained by their actions. That opioid antagonists such as naloxone reverse the analgesic effects of acupuncture further strengthens this hypothesis. Stimulation by acupuncture may also activate the hypothalamus and the pituitary gland, resulting in a broad spectrum of systemic effects. Alteration in the secretion of neurotransmitters and neurohormones and changes in the regulation of blood flow, both centrally and peripherally, have been documented. There is also evidence of alterations in immune functions produced by acupuncture. Which of these and other physiological changes mediate clinical effects is at present unclear.

Despite considerable efforts to understand the anatomy and physiology of the "acupuncture points," the definition and characterization of these points remain controversial. Even more elusive is the scientific basis of some of the key traditional Eastern medical concepts such as the circulation of Qi, the meridian system, and other related theories, which are difficult to reconcile with contemporary biomedical information but continue to play an important role in the evaluation of patients and the formulation of treatment in acupuncture.

The Origins of Acupuncture

The Chinese believed that energy, which they called *chi*, flows from one organ to another during the course of each day. This energy was thought to travel in pathways called *meridians*, which connected the organs. It was discovered that during part of its length each meridian comes near the surface of the body, and that on each meridian there are points of particularly strong activity. Acupuncturists learned to stimulate these points with pressure from their fingers (acupressure), with metal or bone needles inserted to a depth ranging from one or two millimeters to one or two inches (acupuncture), and with heated herbs, which were applied directly to the skin or attached to the needles (moxibustion).

Nobody knows how the Chinese originally discovered these points or mapped out the meridians on which they lay. One legend has it that some warriors who had been injured by arrows and spears had unexpected improvements of chronic physical problems. The Chinese physicians observed the connections between the points of injury by these sharp instruments and the internal organs that were improved, and then asked a number of wise men to meditate on these connections. The result of their meditation was the map of the 14 major meridians and the more than 360 major acupuncture points that are still used today.

James S. Gordon, *Holistic Medicine*, 2001.

Some of the biological effects of acupuncture have also been observed when "sham" acupuncture points are stimulated, highlighting the importance of defining appropriate control groups in assessing biological changes purported to be due to acupuncture. Such findings raise questions regarding the specificity of these biological changes. In addition, similar biological alterations, including the release of endogenous opioids and changes in blood pressure, have been observed after painful stimuli, vigorous exercise, and/or relaxation training; it is at present unclear to what extent acupuncture shares similar biological mechanisms.

It should be noted also that for any therapeutic intervention, including acupuncture, the so-called "non-specific" effects account for a substantial proportion of its effectiveness and thus should not be casually discounted. Many factors may profoundly determine therapeutic outcome, including the quality of the relationship between the clinician and the patient, the degree of trust, the expectations of the patient, the compatibility of the backgrounds and belief systems of the clinician and the patient, as well as a myriad of factors that together define the therapeutic milieu.

Although much remains unknown regarding the mechanism(s) that might mediate the therapeutic effect of acupuncture, the panel is encouraged that a number of significant acupuncture-related biological changes can be identified and carefully delineated. Further research in this direction not only is important for elucidating the phenomena associated with acupuncture, but also has the potential for exploring new pathways in human physiology not previously examined in a systematic manner. . . .

The Promising Future of Acupuncture

Acupuncture as a therapeutic intervention is widely practiced in the United States. There have been many studies of its potential usefulness. However, many of these studies provide equivocal results because of design, sample size, and other factors. The issue is further complicated by inherent difficulties in the use of appropriate controls, such as placebo and sham acupuncture groups.

However, promising results have emerged, for example, efficacy of acupuncture in adult postoperative and chemotherapy nausea and vomiting and in postoperative dental pain. There are other situations such as addiction, stroke rehabilitation, headache, menstrual cramps, tennis elbow, fibromyalgia, myofascial pain, osteoarthritis, low back pain, carpal tunnel syndrome, and asthma for which acupuncture may be useful as an adjunct treatment or an acceptable alternative or be included in a comprehensive management program. Further research is likely to uncover additional areas where acupuncture interventions will be useful.

Findings from basic research have begun to elucidate the

mechanisms of action of acupuncture, including the release of opioids and other peptides in the central nervous system and the periphery and changes in neuroendocrine function. Although much needs to be accomplished, the emergence of plausible mechanisms for the therapeutic effects of acupuncture is encouraging.

The introduction of acupuncture into the choice of treatment modalities readily available to the public is in its early stages. Issues of training, licensure, and reimbursement remain to be clarified. There is sufficient evidence, however, of its potential value to conventional medicine to encourage further studies.

There is sufficient evidence of acupuncture's value to expand its use into conventional medicine and to encourage further studies of its physiology and clinical value.

"Acupuncture is an unproven modality of treatment."

The Effectiveness of Acupuncture Has Not Been Proven

Stephen Barrett

In the following viewpoint, Stephen Barrett claims that acupuncture has not been proven to work, despite the claims of advocates of traditional Chinese medicine. According to Barrett, studies conclude that acupuncture does not relieve pain better than placebos do. He contends that rather than support the use of acupuncture, the National Institutes of Health should point out the treatment's drawbacks. Barrett is vice president of the National Council Against Health Fraud, a scientific adviser to the American Council on Science and Health, and the author of forty-nine books, including *The Health Robbers: A Close Look at Quackery in America*.

As you read, consider the following questions:

1. According to Barrett, how is acupuncture used in Chinese surgery?
2. What is the "fake needle" test, as described by the author?
3. What problem does Barrett believe the National Institutes of Health should have emphasized in its report?

Excerpted from "Acupuncture, Qigong, and 'Chinese Medicine,'" by Stephen Barrett, *Quackwatch*, September 2, 2001. Copyright © 2001 by Stephen Barrett. Reprinted with permission.

Traditional acupuncture, as now practiced, involves the insertion of stainless steel needles into various body areas. A low-frequency current may be applied to the needles to produce greater stimulation. Other procedures used separately or together with acupuncture include: moxibustion (burning of floss or herbs applied to the skin); injection of sterile water, procaine, morphine, vitamins, or homeopathic solutions through the inserted needles; applications of laser beams (laserpuncture); placement of needles in the external ear (auriculotherapy); and acupressure (use of manual pressure). Treatment is applied to "acupuncture points," which are said to be located throughout the body. Originally there were 365 such points, corresponding to the days of the year, but the number identified by proponents during the past 2,000 years has increased gradually to about 2,000. Some practitioners place needles at or near the site of disease, whereas others select points on the basis of symptoms.

Traditional Approaches

In traditional acupuncture, a combination of points is usually used. Qigong is also claimed to influence the flow of "vital energy." Internal Qigong involves deep breathing, concentration, and relaxation techniques used by individuals for themselves. External Qigong is performed by "Qigong masters" who claim to cure a wide variety of diseases with energy released from their fingertips. However, scientific investigators of Qigong masters in China have found no evidence of paranormal powers and some evidence of deception. They found, for example, that a patient lying on a table about eight feet from a Qigong master moved rhythmically or thrashed about as the master moved his hands. But when she was placed so that she could no longer see him, her movements were unrelated to his. Falun gong, which China banned, is a Qigong variant claimed to be "a powerful mechanism for healing, stress relief and health improvements."

Most acupuncturists espouse the traditional Chinese view of health and disease and consider acupuncture, herbal medicine, and related practices to be valid approaches to the full gamut of disease. Others reject the traditional approach and merely claim that acupuncture offers a simple way to achieve pain relief. The diagnostic process used by traditional Chinese medicine (TCM) practitioners may include questioning (medical history, lifestyle), observations (skin, tongue, color), listening (breathing sounds), and pulse-taking. Six pulse aspects said to correlate with body organs or functions are checked on each wrist to determine which meridians are "deficient" in chi. (Medical science recognizes only one pulse, corresponding to the heartbeat, which can be felt in the wrist, neck, feet, and various other places.) Some acupuncturists state that the electrical properties of the body may become imbalanced weeks or even months before symptoms occur. These practitioners claim that acupuncture can be used to treat conditions when the patient just "doesn't feel right," even though no disease is apparent. TCM (as well as the folk medical practices of various other Asian countries) is a threat to certain animal species. For example, black bears—valued for their gall bladders—have been hunted nearly to extinction in Asia, and poaching of black bears is a growing problem in North America.

Dubious Claims

The conditions claimed to respond to acupuncture include chronic pain (neck and back pain, migraine headaches), acute injury-related pain (strains, muscle and ligament tears), gastrointestinal problems (indigestion, ulcers, constipation, diarrhea), cardiovascular conditions (high and low blood pressure), genitourinary problems (menstrual irregularity, frigidity, impotence), muscle and nerve conditions (paralysis, deafness), and behavioral problems (overeating, drug dependence, smoking). However, the evidence supporting these claims consists mostly of practitioners' observations and poorly designed studies. A controlled study found that electroacupuncture of the ear was no more effective than placebo stimulation (light touching) against chronic pain. In 1990, three Dutch epidemiologists [Paul Knipschild, Gerben ter Reit, and Jos Kleijnen] analyzed 51 controlled studies of acupuncture for chronic pain and concluded that "the quality of even the better studies proved to be mediocre. . . . The efficacy of acupuncture in the treatment of chronic pain remains doubtful." They also examined reports of acupuncture used to treat addictions to cigarettes, heroin, and alcohol, and concluded that claims that acupuncture is effective as a therapy for these conditions are not supported by sound clinical research.

Acupuncture anesthesia is not used for surgery in the Orient to the extent that its proponents suggest. In China physicians screen out patients who appear to be unsuitable. Acupuncture is not used for emergency surgery and often is accompanied by local anesthesia or narcotic medication.

A Tricky Business

Promising as the research [on acupuncture] is, experts are quick to point out its scientific shortcomings. One major limitation is the difficulty of discerning whether the procedure itself helps patients or whether the powerful placebo effect is at work. Consider that compared with conventional Western doctors, who are often chided for their revolving-door treatment and uncommunicative dealings with their patients, acupuncturists often spend more time talking with their patients—treatments average 45 minutes to an hour—and carry out their work in a soothing atmosphere unlike the doctor's office.

What's more, the yardstick by which acupuncture is judged in many clinical studies—perception of pain—is itself a gray area, since one person's incapacitating pain may be another's minor interference. Thus, compared with, say, seeing whether a drug brings down a cholesterol level, determining whether acupuncture relieves pain is tricky business.

Tufts University Health & Nutrition Letter, June 1998.

How acupuncture may relieve pain is unclear. One theory suggests that pain impulses are blocked from reaching the spinal cord or brain at various "gates" to these areas. Another theory suggests that acupuncture stimulates the body to produce narcotic-like substances called endorphins, which reduce pain. Other theories suggest that the placebo effect, external suggestion (hypnosis), and cultural conditioning are important factors. [Ronald] Melzack and [Patrick] Wall note that pain relief produced by acupuncture can also be produced by many other types of sensory hyperstimulation, such as electricity and heat at acupuncture points and elsewhere in the body. They conclude that "the effectiveness of all of these forms of stimulation indicates that acupuncture is not a magical procedure but only one of many ways to produce analgesia [pain relief] by an intense sensory input." In 1981, the American Medical Association Council on Scientific Affairs noted that pain relief does not occur consistently or reproducibly in most people and does not operate at all in some people.

In 1995, George A. Ulett, M.D., Ph.D., Clinical Professor of Psychiatry, University of Missouri School of Medicine, stated that "devoid of metaphysical thinking, acupuncture becomes a rather simple technique that can be useful as a nondrug method of pain control." He believes that the traditional Chinese variety is primarily a placebo treatment, but electrical stimulation of about 80 acupuncture points has been proven useful for pain control.

The quality of TCM research in China has been extremely poor. A recent analysis of 2,938 reports of clinical trials reported in Chinese medical journals concluded that no conclusions could be drawn from the vast majority of them. The researchers stated:

> In most of the trials, disease was defined and diagnosed according to conventional medicine; trial outcomes were assessed with objective or subjective (or both) methods of conventional medicine, often complemented by traditional Chinese methods. Over 90% of the trials in non-specialist journals evaluated herbal treatments that were mostly proprietary Chinese medicines. . . .

> Although methodological quality has been improving over the years, many problems remain. The method of randomisation was often inappropriately described. Blinding was used in only 15% of trials. Only a few studies had sample sizes of 300 subjects or more. Many trials used as a control another Chinese medicine treatment whose effectiveness had often not been evaluated by randomised controlled trials. Most trials focused on short term or intermediate rather than long term outcomes. Most trials did not report data on compliance and completeness of follow up. Effectiveness was rarely quantitatively expressed and reported. Intention to treat analysis was never mentioned. Over half did not report data on baseline characteristics or on side effects. Many trials were published as short reports. Most trials claimed that the tested

treatments were effective, indicating that publication bias may be common; a funnel plot of the 49 trials of acupuncture in the treatment of stroke confirmed selective publication of positive trials in the area, suggesting that acupuncture may not be more effective than the control treatments.

Two scientists at the University of Heidleberg have developed a "fake needle" that may enable acupuncture researchers to perform better-designed controlled studies. The device is a needle with a blunt tip that moves freely within a copper handle. When the tip touches the skin, the patient feels a sensation similar to that of an acupuncture needle. At the same time, the visible part of the needle moves inside the handle so it appears to shorten as though penetrating the skin. When the device was tested on volunteers, none suspected that it had not penetrated the skin. . . .

Useless Certification

The National Certification Commission for Acupuncture and Oriental Medicine (NCCAOM) has set voluntary certification standards and certified several thousand practitioners. As of November 1998, 32 states have licensing laws, with 29 of them using NCCAOM examination as all or part of their educational, training, or examination requirement, and three with additional eligibility criteria. The credentials used by acupuncturists include C.A. (certified acupuncturist), Lic. Ac. (licensed acupuncturist), M.A. (master acupuncturist), Dip. Ac. (diplomate of acupuncture), and O.M.D. (doctor of Oriental medicine). Some of these have legal significance, but they do not signify that the holder is competent to make adequate diagnoses or render appropriate treatment. In 1990, the U.S. Secretary of Education recognized what is now called the Accreditation Commission for Acupuncture and Oriental Medicine (ACAOM) as an accrediting agency. However, such recognition is not based on the scientific validity of what is taught but upon other criteria. [George] Ulett has noted:

> Certification of acupuncturists is a sham. While a few of those so accredited are naive physicians, most are nonmedical persons who only play at being doctor and use this certification as an umbrella for a host of unproven New Age hokum treatments. Unfortunately, a few HMOs, hospitals,

and even medical schools are succumbing to the bait and exposing patients to such bogus treatments when they need real medical care.

The National Council Against Health Fraud (NCAHF) has concluded:

Acupuncture is an unproven modality of treatment. Its theory and practice are based on primitive and fanciful concepts of health and disease that bear no relationship to present scientific knowledge. Research during the past 20 years has not demonstrated that acupuncture is effective against any disease.

Perceived effects of acupuncture are probably due to a combination of expectation, suggestion, counter-irritation, conditioning, and other psychologic mechanisms.

The use of acupuncture should be restricted to appropriate research settings.

Insurance companies should not be required by law to cover acupuncture treatment.

Licensure of lay acupuncturists should be phased out.

Consumers who wish to try acupuncture should discuss their situation with a knowledgeable physician who has no commercial interest.

An Inadequate NIH Report

In 1997, a Consensus Development Conference sponsored by the National Institutes of Health and several other agencies concluded that "there is sufficient evidence . . . of acupuncture's value to expand its use into conventional medicine and to encourage further studies of its physiology and clinical value." The panelists also suggested that the federal government and insurance companies expand coverage of acupuncture so more people can have access to it. These conclusions were not based on research done after NCAHF's position paper was published. Rather, they reflected the bias of the panelists who were selected by a planning committee dominated by acupuncture proponents. NCAHF board chairman Wallace Sampson, M.D., has described the conference "a consensus of proponents, not a consensus of valid scientific opinion."

Although the report described some serious problems, it failed to place them into proper perspective. The panel acknowledged that "the vast majority of papers studying acupuncture consist of case reports, case series, or intervention studies with designs inadequate to assess efficacy" and that "relatively few" high-quality controlled trials have been published about acupuncture's effects. But it reported that "the World Health Organization has listed more than 40 [conditions] for which [acupuncture] may be indicated." This sentence should have been followed by a statement that the list was not valid. Far more serious, although the consensus report touched on Chinese acupuncture theory, it failed to point out the danger and economic waste involved in going to practitioners who can't make appropriate diagnoses. The report noted:

> The general theory of acupuncture is based on the premise that there are patterns of energy flow (Qi) through the body that are essential for health. Disruptions of this flow are believed to be responsible for disease. The acupuncturist can correct imbalances of flow at identifiable points close to the skin.

> Acupuncture focuses on a holistic, energy-based approach to the patient rather than a disease-oriented diagnostic and treatment model.

> Despite considerable efforts to understand the anatomy and physiology of the "acupuncture points," the definition and characterization of these points remains controversial. Even more elusive is the scientific basis of some of the key traditional Eastern medical concepts such as the circulation of Qi, the meridian system, and the five phases theory, which are difficult to reconcile with contemporary biomedical information but continue to play an important role in the evaluation of patients and the formulation of treatment in acupuncture.

Simply stated, this means that if you go to a practitioner who practices traditional Chinese medicine, you are unlikely to be properly diagnosed. In 1998, following his lecture at a local college, an experienced TCM practitioner diagnosed me by taking my pulse and looking at my tongue. He stated that my pulse showed signs of "stress" and that my tongue indicated I was suffering from "congestion of the blood." A few minutes later, he examined a woman and told her that her pulse showed premature ventricular contractions (a disturbance of the heart's rhythm that could be harmless or significant, depending on whether the individual has underlying heart disease). He suggested that both of us undergo treatment with acupuncture and herbs—which would have cost about $90 per visit. I took the woman's pulse and found that it was completely normal. I believe that the majority of nonmedical acupuncturists rely on improper diagnostic procedures. The NIH consensus panel should have emphasized the seriousness of this problem.

| *"The fact that [homeopathic] remedies do indeed work is indisputable."*

Homeopathy Is an Effective Treatment

Rudolph Ballentine

Homeopathy is an alternative remedy based on the premise that a patient will be cured if he or she is given minute doses of natural substances that in larger quantities would produce symptoms of the disease being treated. In the following viewpoint, Rudolph Ballentine asserts that homeopathic medicine is effective in treating numerous diseases. However, Ballentine argues that mainstream medical scientists and doctors refuse to accept the results of many studies that have proven homeopathy's effectiveness. Ballentine is the chief medical advisor of the Olive Leaf Wholeness Center in New York City and a professor of psychiatry at Louisiana State University in New Orleans.

As you read, consider the following questions:
1. According to the author, what are the effects of belladonna?
2. How does Ballentine support his contention that homeopathy is scientific?
3. How did *Calcarea mur* affect the author?

Homeopathic medicine takes [the] principle of treating like with like and runs with it. If coffee leaves one wide awake and wired, what do you do for someone who can't stop his busy mind long enough to sleep? You give him potentized coffee. [Potentization is the process of dilution and vigorous shaking by which homeopathic remedies are prepared. Serial potentization is when that process is repeated, up to as many as 100,000 times.] In fact, I have found *Coffea* 200C [Coffea is an evergreen shrub most noted for its aromatic bean. 200C means that one part of the coffee was diluted in 99 parts of ethyl alcohol or distilled water and vigorously shaken, with the process repeated 200 times.] to be a very reliable remedy for insomnia—*if* you have the characteristic hyperalertness that goes with coffee. If you're restless but drowsy—not wide awake—forget it; *Coffea* won't help. The higher you go with the potentization process, the more important it is to match the symptoms accurately, or you'll get no results. In order to uncover the picture of what a remedy will treat, homeopaths have spent the last two hundred years cataloging what natural substances will do when given to healthy persons.

The symptoms produced when a normal subject takes an active herb is called a "proving." *Belladonna* ("deadly nightshade"), for example, in its crude or herbal form, will dilate the pupils and flush the face. This is the reason for its name, which means "beautiful lady." Clever courtesans would swallow tiny amounts from a jeweled medicine box to make their eyes deep and limpid and their cheeks rosy. But if they took more than a little, they would wind up with a pounding headache. Belladonna is toxic. So when you complain to a homeopath of a pounding headache and you also have a red face and dilated pupils, you'll most likely get a dose of *Belladonna*.

The Practice of Homeopathy

Though numbers of lovely ladies in bygone times have offered us what amounted to countless informal "provings" of belladonna, the use of *Belladonna* in clinical homeopathy today is much more sophisticated and is based on many carefully controlled provings using the potentized remedy. In contrast to the plain herb, the potency will produce subtler effects, such as those that are psychological. These are exhaustive, double-blind studies in which some "provers" are given *Belladonna* and others a placebo. Even by the late nineteenth century, enough of this data had been compiled to publish a hefty volume of provings cataloging the symptoms of *Belladonna*. The practice of homeopathy is based on such data.

Here's how it's done: After the substance is given to a healthy person, he or she carefully records the symptoms that result. These symptoms are sorted and ranked. Symptoms that occur repeatedly are considered strong indications for that remedy. The pattern they form is its profile or "symptom picture."

Sepia, for example, is the ink of a type of squid, long used as a pigment in paints. Dreamy artists absentmindedly moistening their brushes with their mouths may have developed the common darkness of mood we often associate with painters as a result of ingesting sepia. When given in potentized form to provers, *Sepia* produces a sagging tiredness and a depressed demeanor. When someone complains of that same pattern of symptoms, you give them *Sepia*. In other words, what causes the symptoms in a healthy person will cure them in one who's sick. This is a very simple, straightforward principle, and there is no theory involved here. It is pure, empirical science.

When [Samuel] Hahnemann articulated the basic principles of the homeopathic method in the late eighteenth century, he was intent on establishing a purely scientific medicine. He expressed his disdain for the "regular" doctors on the one hand, with their bloodletting and violent purges, and the herbalists on the other, with their Doctrine of Signatures, [The "Doctrine of Signatures" is the idea that the purpose of a plant can be determined by observing its color, the shape of its leaf, or where it grows.] which he felt was much abused. (One's fanciful imagination, he maintained— and there was a good measure of truth in what he said— could lead one to see the "signature" of whatever might be convenient!) He wanted instead an approach to treatment that was clear, concise, and free of the problems that plagued most of medicine.

Proving the Effectiveness of Homeopathy

One of those problems is the thorny issue of diagnosis. . . . A number of studies have shown that conventional medical diagnoses are frequently in error. Unfortunately, choices of drugs or surgery are based on those diagnoses. Moreover, both the diagnosis and its treatment are subject to changes in perspective—hence, much of what was done a decade or two ago has since been discredited. The awkward task of moving from a questionable diagnosis to an equally questionable (though currently fashionable) medication is avoided when one follows rigorous homeopathic principles.

When a single homeopathic remedy, developed and prescribed on the basis of provings, is matched to a particular disorder, we essentially eliminate the need for diagnosis. It is the symptom picture observed in the patient that dictates the choice of the remedy. The picture we are treating has emerged in double-blind provings of the remedy. It has been shown again and again that when the remedy is given to a patient who has symptoms like those arising from the provings, resolution and reorganization will result. This is straightforward and empirical.

Despite this, you will hear mainstream professionals say that homeopathy has not been proven, that it is not scientific. What should really be said about homeopathy is that it is not conventional; it is not following currently familiar patterns of drug use. In fact, it is quite thoroughly scientific—not only in the sense that it is solidly based on empirical reasoning—but also because many studies have been done to investigate its effectiveness.

In 1991 the *British Medical Journal* published an extensive review article by a group of researchers in Holland on the efficacy of homeopathy. Those researchers had gone back and pulled out all the literature published in reputable medical journals on the subject, planning, it seems, to lay this issue of homeopathy to rest once and for all. They found 107 clinical trials that had been published. Seventy-seven percent of those trials showed that homeopathy worked. So they evaluated the methodology used, to see how carefully the trials were conducted. They expected to find that the studies that showed homeopathy to be effective would be the ones most sloppily performed—not good science. Instead, to their surprise, they found that in a clear majority of those more rigorous studies, homeopathy proved effective. They commented, "Based on this evidence we would be ready to accept that homeopathy can be efficacious, if only the mechanism of action were more plausible. . . ."

Resistance to Homeopathy

And there's the rub. The evidence is there, but it is ignored because of the difficulty we have in accepting that nonmaterial remedies [Nonmaterial refers to the idea that the body has the innate wisdom needed to heal itself.] can heal. The implications of that proposition are so mind-boggling that most mainstream medical scientists, with their stubbornly materialistic orientation, simply do not want to hear about it. The principles demonstrated by homeopathy will throw into question that majority of our scientific assumptions, which are based on the primacy of matter. Rather than open this Pandora's box, the medical scientist simply thrusts his head in the sand and dismisses homeopathy altogether.

This resistance is not new. It has been in evidence since the rediscovery of the homeopathic principle by Hahnemann in the late eighteenth century. The early successes of homeopathy were not embraced by the conventional medicine of that day, either. In 1813, for example, when the remnants of Napoleon's defeated army drifted back from Russia, bringing typhus with them, an epidemic broke out in Leipzig that gave the emerging homeopaths an opportunity to test their method. By that time they had two remedies that seemed to cover the symptoms of the disease: fever, pain, and debility. One of them, however, *Rhus tox* (poison oak), was characterized by restlessness. (If you've ever had a bad case of poison oak, you may remember the extreme restlessness that accompanies the rash.) The other remedy, *Bryonia*, had shown in its proving a quite opposite tendency: provers wanted to lie down, not move, and be left alone. If bothered, they could be quite irritable.

During the epidemic, these early homeopaths simply applied one of these two remedies—*Rhus tox* or *Bryonia*—depending on whether the patient was restless or wanted to lie still. This was a rather primitive approach to prescribing, but it worked. Out of 183 treated, only one elderly patient died, although in those days typhus usually killed half of those afflicted. This created quite a stir. Similar dramatic results followed in the 1830s, as cholera began to plague Europe.

When the cholera epidemic reached England, it provided another opportunity to compare homeopathic treatment with the conventional methods of the day. Regular allopathic medicine yielded a mortality rate of 59 percent compared to only 16 percent for the homeopaths. When these statistics were collected, the information was so startling that a medical commission was sent to the London Homeopathic Hospital to check the records. Though the data were duly verified, it was decided not to make them public, and the facts were not released until a hundred years later.

Scientific Responses to Homeopathy

Lest we be scornful of such suppression of information, we should acknowledge that the homeopathic pill is a hard one to swallow. Not literally, of course. In fact, it's a pleasant-tasting little pellet of milk sugar. But the concept is one to choke on. Our fixation on the world of matter makes it difficult to grasp the idea that a nonmaterial medicinal could be of any use, and with homeopathic remedies above the 12x, there is no *substance* left. After that many serial potentization steps, there is, statistically, only one chance in a million that even *one molecule* of the original material from which the remedy was made is left. There's nothing there. There's information there, but there's no *thing* there. [A medicine that is labeled 12x was diluted in a 1:9 ratio, with the process repeated twelve times.]

This is why scientists, with their limited conceptual repertoire, discounted homeopathy and concluded *a priori* that it was absurd. This is in contrast to herbal medicine, where researchers can feel comfortable with the idea that it might work if they can identify the "active ingredient" and understand its action the way they understand a drug. But there's no way you can stuff homeopathy into a materialistic paradigm. It won't fit, and the dyed-in-the-wool materialist can only insist stubbornly that it can't work. Never mind that people get better—even get well—after they take the remedies, it simply *can't work!* This is, of course, where we cease to be scientific—when we shy away from observations that don't fit our notion of how things should be. The true scientist, by contrast, delights in the "aberrant observation," the event that can't be explained by current theory. He senses that it's the key to tantalizing discoveries that lie just over the horizon. It's the doorway to a new world.

Commonly Used Homeopathic Remedies

Arsenicum	restless but weak and exhausted; fearful, selfish; burning pains better from heat; thin excoriating discharges
Belladonna	flushed face, dilated pupils; near delirium, headache worse from sudden movement
Bryonia	just wants to be left alone; everything worse from motion; mucous membranes all dry
Carbo veg	incomplete oxidation; weak digestion, bad gas; cold sweat, craves air
Merc sol	swollen glands, thick indented tongue; copious sweat that fails to relieve; sensitive to heat *and* cold
Nux vom	ill-tempered adrenaline junkie; stomach irritated by stimulants; miscellaneous ailments from stress
Pulsatilla	weepy, changeable, contradictory; chilly but better outdoors; rarely thirsty; copious bland discharges
Rhus tox	restless but stiff and painful on starting to move ("the rusty hinge"); worse cold or wet

Rudolph Ballentine, "Radical Healing," 1999.

But we don't always remain true to the spirit of science. More often we get stuck in the comfort of the familiar—however boring and counterproductive that may become. We don't want to be jarred loose. It's the same mentality as the first person to experience [Alexander Graham] Bell's telephone. "Where is he? There's no one here, and yet I hear a voice in my ear!" It was too much of a stretch. Mark Twain, with his concrete Missouri stubborness, refused to buy homeopathy. He said—and we can picture him shaking his head—"It's the soup made from the shadow of a pigeon's wing."

A Personal Experience

I was hard put to believe that there was anything to it myself. After I began practicing homeopathy and prescribing remedies to my patients, I still clung to some skepticism—the residue, perhaps of my allopathic [Allopathy is the term commonly used to describe Western medicine, particularly the use of surgeries and treatments that are specifically targeted to a disease.] medical training. When patients told me they got better from the remedies, I would ask, almost surprised, "You did? Are you sure?" So when my teacher suggested a deep-acting remedy he felt was especially suited to me—*Calcarea mur* 1M, I was not expecting much.

I went to the pharmacy I had set up in the utility room next to my kitchen, and put a drop of the remedy on a dab of powdered lactose and let it fall under my tongue. I didn't make it halfway across the kitchen before it occurred to me that perhaps I should sit down. There was no chair, so I sat on the floor. Then it struck me that it might feel even better to lie down. I did so, and lay there on the floor, staring at the ceiling. I felt strangely wonderful. Subtle currents seemed to be moving inside me—in a way that was pleasant, yet totally unfamiliar. Getting up seemed not only overly ambitious but altogether unreasonable. I was very content to lie quietly and stare overhead.

In the morning my assistant found me still lying there, staring at the ceiling, where the light was on. This bit of nothing I had ingested had totally reorganized my energy body. It wasn't that I was disabled; it was simply that moving was such a radically new experience that I was overwhelmed by the prospect. So I had just lain there all night. After that experience, I was a complete believer. I am sure that remedies had had an effect on me before this incident, but if they had, I had not been tuned into their action. I had to be hit over the head to really get it.

It's less difficult to believe today. Intelligent stuff is finally beginning to be written about homeopathy. Water molecules have the ability to shape themselves around each other and around other molecules in very complex ways. The intricate assemblage that results, researchers are now beginning to suspect, might carry a wealth of information. When we shake our bit of sulfur, for example, in a tube to make a homeopathic remedy, perhaps the alcohol that is mixed with the water in some way facilitates the imprinting of information about the sulfur onto that water. This might explain why it is that by the time we've finished, we have a highly charged solution with lots and lots of information, even though nothing remains of the original sulfur from which the information was derived.

This is the most promising perspective to date on how the homeopathic remedy might have its amazing effects. But the truth is that, at least for now, this theory remains a matter of speculation. Nevertheless, the fact that the remedies do indeed work is indisputable. The evidence on that is in, and the method for harnessing this healing power has been well articulated and is quite simple: (1) pin down the patient's symptom picture, and (2) match that to the symptoms of the remedy (that come from provings).

| "*Pending further evidence, homeopathy remains a form of placebo therapy.*"

Homeopathy Does Not Work

David W. Ramey

Homeopathy is a method of treating diseases with minute quantities of substances that would produce symptoms similar to the disease being treated if administered in larger quantities. David W. Ramey maintains in the following viewpoint that numerous studies have proven that these homeopathic remedies fail to cure illnesses and can worsen a patient's condition. According to Ramey, these studies have concluded that homeopathy provides only a placebo effect, or the positive response a patient has to a treatment regardless of whether or not the remedy is actually efficacious. Ramey is a veterinarian who specializes in equine medicine and has written nine books on equine health.

As you read, consider the following questions:

1. What were the conclusions of a 1990 French review of homeopathy studies, as cited by Ramey?
2. What is a "serial agitated dilution," as defined by the author?
3. According to Ramey, what are three of the ailments that are not improved by homeopathic treatment?

The scientific investigations of homeopathy that have been completed and published are sufficient for drawing reliable conclusions about this counterscientific approach to medicine. These studies have generated widely assorted positive, negative, and neutral conclusions. Therefore, it is not difficult, especially if one does not consider the quality of the evidence, to find published conclusions compatible with, or pervertible to, a particular bias. But parading pieces of evidence thus culled does the public little or no good.

A Survey of Homeopathy Studies

A sensible short-cut to taking on the question of whether homeopathy is effective is to examine all relevant published reports of meta-analytic studies (statistical studies of studies) and of other scientific reviews. This approach is not without drawbacks, however. In a meta-analytic study, for example, an explicit and straightforward conclusion may be based on the findings of weak (e.g., poorly designed) studies.

Homeopathy has been the subject of at least 12 scientific reviews, including meta-analytic studies, published since the mid-1980s. From reading the literature that proponents of homeopathy disseminate, one might well get the impression that the findings of these studies are somewhat open to interpretation, and that the basic question regarding the evidence amounts to: "Is the glass half empty, or half full?" But the findings are remarkably consistent:

• In a 1990 French review of 40 published randomized clinical trials of homeopathy, researchers found that most of the studies had had major methodological flaws and concluded: ". . . the results do not provide acceptable evidence that homeopathic treatments are effective."

• In a meta-analytic study of homeopathy in human medicine published in the *British Medical Journal* in 1991, investigators concluded: "At the moment the evidence of clinical trials is positive but not sufficient to draw definitive conclusions because most trials are of low methodological quality and because of the unknown role of publication bias. This indicates that there is a legitimate case for further evaluation of homeopathy, but only by means of well-performed trials."

• In a 1992 German review of homeopathy in human

medicine, researchers concluded: ". . . The review of studies carried out according to current scientific criteria revealed—at best—a placebo effect of homeopathy. Until now there is no proven mechanism for the mode of action of homeopathy. Sometimes so-called alternative medicine prevents effective curative measures. . . ."

• In a 1993 German review of homeopathy in veterinary medicine, researchers came to several conclusions: (*a*) "Doctor and veterinarian are similarly obligated to apply the therapeutic measure that prevailing opinions deem most effective. Where there is for particular definite illnesses a particularly effective and generally recognized treatment, in such cases the supporters of homeopathy may not disregard the better successes from their own differing direction." (*b*) "It is undisputed that homeopathy in the area of stronger potency can achieve effects pharmacologically and toxicologically; the superiority of homeopathy as a therapeutic measure in comparison with conventional therapy methods is at this point not verified. Moreover, the harmlessness of homeopathy in stronger potency is for the most part not verified." (*c*) "The effectiveness of homeopathy in middle and high potencies is up to now not verified. It is undisputed that with the help of homeopathy, not insignificant placebo effects can be achieved. In veterinary medicine, giving an animal an 'active' placebo and another a 'passive' can play a significant role and influence the owner."

Homeopathy and Placebo Therapy

• Every standard homeopathic preparation is a serial agitated dilution (SAD)—that is, a result of the successive admixture and agitation of a substance. In a 1994 review and meta-analytic study of SADs in experimental toxicology, investigators stated: "As with clinical studies, the overall quality of toxicology research using SAD preparations is low. The majority of studies either could not be reevaluated by the reviewers or were of such low quality that their likelihood of validity is doubtful. The number of methodologically sound, independently reproduced studies is too small to make any definitive conclusions regarding the effect of SAD preparations in toxicology."

• In a 1996 French review of homeopathy, researchers made the following statements. (*a*) "No one should ignore the role of nonspecific factors in therapeutic efficacy, such as the natural history of a given disease and the placebo effect. Indeed, these factors can be used to therapeutic advantage." (*b*) "As homeopathic treatments are generally used in conditions with variable outcome or showing spontaneous recovery (hence their placebo responsiveness), these treatments are widely considered to have an effect in some patients." (*c*) "However, despite the large number of comparative trials carried out to date there is no evidence that homeopathy is any more effective than placebo therapy given in identical

---

Contradicting Basic Science

At first glance, the homeopathic principle—that is, the supposition that like cures like, especially in reduced doses—sufficiently resembles mainstream immunization theory to entitle it to a hearing. But one obvious difference is that immunization has a theory behind it that is persuasive in its own terms and congruent with scientific theory in general. By contrast, Samuel Hahnemann [who developed the principles of homeopathy in the eighteenth century] taught that not only is the actual cause of disease unknown, it is unknowable. Perhaps more importantly, homeopathic practice flatly contradicts basic chemistry and physics. According to Hahnemann, the more dilute a homeopathic remedy, the more powerful it will be. The trick, at each stage of dilution, is to "potentize" the medication—by giving it a good shaking. This dictum has led to dilutions so extreme that any given vial of homeopathic medicine may contain not a single molecule of the medicine itself. Instead, it will contain water, plus an unknown concentration of contaminants—animal, mineral, or vegetable.

Advocates of homeopathy have come up with a neat rejoinder to this problem: by a process not understood (and perhaps not to be understood), water somehow "remembers" what it was once mixed with, even after the last molecule has departed. But, unfortunately, there is no evidence for the notion of liquid memories; and, as [Barrie] Cassileth points out, if such memories should somehow be proved to exist, the liquid would presumably have to remember all the various impurities it once contained as well.

Samuel McCracken, *Commentary*, June 1999.

---

conditions." (*d*) "We believe that homeopathic preparations should not be used to treat serious diseases when other drugs are known to be both effective and safe." (*e*) "Pending further evidence, homeopathy remains a form of placebo therapy."

• Of their study published in the *Lancet* in 1997, investigators said: "The results of our meta-analysis are not compatible with the hypothesis that the clinical effects of homeopathy are completely due to placebo. However, we found insufficient evidence from these studies that homeopathy is clearly efficacious for any single clinical condition." They further stated: "Our study has no major implications for clinical practice because we found little evidence of effectiveness of any single homeopathic approach on any single clinical condition." In conclusion the researchers stated that more research on homeopathy was in order "providing it is rigorous and systematic."

(In a later issue, a critic of the study noted that the best of the trials in question had been distinctly less likely to generate a positive finding than had the trials as a whole, and another critic indicated that preferential nonpublication of relevant studies that had generated negative findings may have skewed the findings of the meta-analytic study.)

Ineffective and Dangerous Treatments

• In another meta-analytic study conducted in 1997, researchers examined the use of homeopathy for postoperative ileus, a condition characterized principally by surgical lack of peristalsis and measured by the delay between the close of a surgical procedure and the first post-op expulsion of flatus. The investigators concluded: "[Our analyses] do not provide evidence for the use of a particular homeopathic remedy or for a combination of remedies for postoperative ileus. Several drawbacks inherent in the original studies and in the methodology of meta-analysis preclude a firm conclusion." They also noted that the effect of homeopathic preparations of not more than 12c—i.e., preparations that might contain some of the basic substance—was significant, whereas that of homeopathic preparations of more than 12c was not.

• In a review of homeopathic treatment of animals published in 1998, S.G. Wynn recommended approaching homeopathy with an "open mind." As evidence of efficacy, she cited three studies in which some improvement had been directly observed, seven studies whose data were ambiguous, and six studies in which the animals' condition had worsened or had not changed. In several of these 16 studies, the subjects had been healthy to start with. Wynn even described a study in which the condition of sick animals had worsened as possible evidence of effectiveness through induction of a "healing crisis."

• In a 1998 review of the effects of homeopathic preparations based on the herb arnica, which are typically used to treat conditions due to physical trauma, researchers concluded: "The claim that homeopathic arnica is efficacious beyond a placebo effect is not supported by rigorous clinical trials."

• In a review published in November 1999 of the use of homeopathic "remedies" to prevent headaches, E. Ernst concluded that available trial data do not suggest that homeopathy is more effective than a placebo in the prevention of migraines or other headaches.

• In a meta-analytic study published in January 2000, it was found that a homeopathic preparation for preventing colds and the flu was ineffective.

Several rigorous trials of homeopathy in human medicine have been performed in recent years. According to these randomized, placebo-controlled, double-blind trials, homeopathic "remedies" are not effective:

- in the treatment of adenoid vegetations (abnormal glandular growths) in children,
- for controlling pain and infection after a total abdominal hysterectomy, and
- for preventing migraines.

Furthermore, none of the studies that have generated positive findings has been replicated with such findings, the methodological quality of these studies has been questionable, and the better studies of homeopathy have tended not to generate positive findings.

Periodical Bibliography

The following articles have been selected to supplement the diverse views presented in this chapter.

Marcia Angell and Jerome P. Kassirer	"Alternative Medicine—the Risks of Untested and Unregulated Remedies," *New England Journal of Medicine*, September 17, 1998.
Beth Baker	"The Faith Factor," *Common Boundary*, July/August 1997.
Dawn Baumann Brunke	"Think Yourself Well," *Fate*, July 1998.
Dana Canedy	"Real Medicine or Medicine Show?" *New York Times*, July 23, 1998.
Ronald W. Dworkin	"Science, Faith, and Alternative Medicine," *Policy Review*, August/September 2001.
Evelyn Gilbert	"Good Vibrations," *Village Voice*, July 29, 1997.
David Hicks	"Science or Superstition?" *World & I*, March 1998.
Megan A. Johnson	"Homeopathy: Another Tool in the Bag," *Journal of the American Medical Association*, March 4, 1998.
Kevin Paraino	"The Truth About Nontraditional Treatments," *Newsweek*, September 3, 2001.
Robert L. Park	"Alternative Medicine and the Laws of Physics," *Skeptical Inquirer*, September/October 1997.
Jack Raso	"Is There a Cure for Alternative Medicine?" *Priorities*, vol. 9, no. 2, 1997.
Barry F. Seidman	"Will Alternative and Mainstream Medicine Ever Be Friends?" *Skeptical Inquirer*, January 2001.
Karen Stabiner	"With Alternative Medicine, Profits Are Big, Rules Are Few," *New York Times*, June 21, 1998.
Stephanie Stapleton	"Alternative Medicine: Time to Talk," *American Medical News*, December 14, 1998.
Chuck Whitlock	"'Natural' Does Not Mean 'Good for You,'" *Consumers' Research Magazine*, September 2001.

CHAPTER 3

Are New Medical Technologies Beneficial?

Chapter Preface

Medical technologies such as in vitro fertilization—the fertilization of a human egg cell in a laboratory, which is then implanted in a woman's womb—and fertility drugs have enabled more women to give birth. In many cases, these technologies result in multiple births, such as the 1985 birth of the Frustaci septuplets, the first septuplets born in the United States. These babies often face serious medical problems, raising questions as to whether increasing a woman's fertility is beneficial.

Multiple-birth babies are typically born prematurely, before their organs and nervous systems have developed completely. Consequently these infants are more likely to have underdeveloped lungs and a greater susceptibility to infections. As they develop, these babies—if they survive—are at an increased risk for learning disabilities. For example, one of Patti Frustaci's septuplets was stillborn and three more died in the next three weeks. The three surviving septuplets were diagnosed with cerebral palsy and mental retardation.

The children of multiple births and their parents suffer emotionally as well. Ezekiel J. Emanuel argues that multiple births "are the product of fertility technology misused—an error, not a wonder." According to Emanuel, who is the chairman of the department of clinical ethics at the National Institutes of Health, children of multiple births suffer emotionally because they do not receive adequate parental attention. Moreover, the parents of these multiples face their own set of problems. Great Britain's Human Fertilisation and Embryology Authority reports that the mothers often experience anxiety, depression, and other emotional problems. These problems can lead to marital troubles; for example, the Frustacis eventually separated.

The potential pitfalls of multiple births have prompted doctors to restrict the number of fertilized eggs they will implant in the womb. Doctors have also begun the use of selective reduction, in which some of the embryos are aborted to ensure that the remaining embryos have a greater chance at survival. However, many women refuse selective reduction on religious grounds.

Fertility technologies have the potential to benefit numerous lives. However, they and other medical breakthroughs also lead to numerous questions as to the safety and potential dangers of these procedures. In the following chapter, the authors consider the advantages and disadvantages of medical technology.

"Solving the organ shortage is a matter of finding an organ source that is plentiful and safe. The most promising source . . . is the pig."

Xenotransplantation Can Solve the Organ Shortage

Peggy Slasman

Xenotransplantation is a process whereby an organ from one species is transplanted into the body of another species; these operations typically involve an animal donor and human recipient. Doctors can safely and effectively replace deteriorating human organs with pig organs, Peggy Slasman argues in the following viewpoint. Slasman maintains that pig organs are viable replacements for human organs because they are similar in size and shape to their human counterparts and are readily available. She also contends that scientists are developing techniques to minimize the risk that the recipient's body will reject the pig organ or become infected by it. Slasman is the chief public relations officer at Massachusetts General Hospital in Boston.

As you read, consider the following questions:

1. In Slasman's opinion, why are fewer ethical concerns raised by the use of pig organs compared to the use of nonhuman primate organs?
2. What is "inducing tolerance," as defined by the author?
3. According to A. Benedict Cosimi, when will widespread acceptance of xenotransplantation occur?

From "Transplantation's Next Frontier," by Peggy Slasman, *Saturday Evening Post*, September/October 1997. Copyright © 1997 by Peggy Slasman. Reprinted with permission.

At this very moment, approximately 50,000 people are on the national waiting list for an organ transplant; only 20,000 of them will receive one. Nearly ten people die each day, waiting and hoping for that lifesaving organ. And those who actually make it onto the waiting list represent only a subset of those who potentially could benefit from organ transplantation.

"We know these patients, and we see them becoming weaker and sicker while they wait for an organ," says A. Benedict Cosimi, M.D., chief of the transplant unit at Boston's Massachusetts General Hospital. "We have the technology and skill to save lives, but we don't have the organs. Too often we stand by helpless and frustrated, watching patients die, seeing families torn apart. If we had enough organs, we could restore lives to patients, preserve families."

The Next Step for Organ Transplantation

Inspired by these patients, Massachusetts General researchers and clinicians are advancing along the path toward what is widely seen as transplantation's next frontier: using organs from animals to replace the failing organs of humans, a technology known as "xenotransplantation."

David H. Sachs, M.D., director of Massachusetts General's Transplantation Biology Research Center (TBRC), has spent more than a quarter century—virtually his entire scientific career—bringing xenotransplantation closer to reality. Along the way, he says, he has learned much about the body's immune response. A deliberate and confident man, Sachs explains that solving the organ shortage is a matter of finding an organ source that is plentiful and safe. The most promising source, he says, is the pig.

The anatomy and physiology of pigs are remarkably similar to those of humans. Their digestive, respiratory, pulmonary, and cardiovascular structures parallel those of humans. And the organs of the specific breed of miniature swine that Sachs has developed over the years are similar in size to human organs, fitting the tiniest newborn baby to adults 300 pounds or greater.

Other benefits of pigs include their early sexual maturation and frequent large litters, enabling rapid production of significant numbers of animals. The pigs are raised in a controlled, clean setting and harbor few or no diseases. Finally, because society has long regarded the pig as food—last year more than 90 million pigs were raised for food—the use of pig organs for transplantation, compared with organs from nonhuman primates, such as baboons, elicits fewer ethical concerns.

Overcoming the Difficulties

Yet transplanting an organ from pig to human is fraught with difficulties. When any nonhuman organ is transplanted into a person, the body recognizes it as foreign.

The immune system swings into overdrive, mounting an attack so fierce, so swift that within minutes the transplanted organ is rendered useless. This intense response is known as "hyperacute rejection." Beyond hyperacute rejection, other immune system warriors, such as the white blood cells, or lymphocytes, stand at the ready to fight off the foreign tissue.

Sachs and his research team are exploring ways to overcome these various phases of rejection. One of the most promising means involves "inducing tolerance," coaxing the recipient's body to accept a donor organ with little or no immunosuppression, keeping immune defenses intact to stave off infection.

"We're achieving success with tolerance right now in the laboratory with same-species kidney transplants," Sachs says, describing animals that have thrived for more than three years with mismatched organs without long-term immunosuppresive drug. "We're also making progress in achieving tolerance in cross-species transplants."

Altering the Immune System

A research team led by Megan Sykes, M.D., has been studying tolerance achieved by first transplanting bone marrow from the donor into the recipient. Bone marrow manufactures white blood cells called B lymphocytes, which produce antibodies that attack alien tissue. Another type of white blood cell called the T lymphocyte, which forms in the thymus, also comes into play in rejection, destroying foreign tissue by attaching itself to antigens from the invader's cells.

By inducing donor and recipient marrow to coexist, Sykes has produced a condition called "mixed chimerism," virtually creating a new immune system that is part recipient, part donor. The reconstituted immune system is tricked into thinking the donor organ actually belongs in the recipient, thus it wages no attack.

Treating Diabetes and Other Diseases

In 1993 transplanted pig islet cells in insulin-dependent diabetics were examined in a clinical trial in Sweden. Under low-power magnification, these cells, first described in the pancreas by Paul Langerhans in 1869, look like clustered islands (hence the name islets) and include cells that make insulin. Results seem to indicate that porcine foetal islet cells can be safely transplanted into diabetics, provided that the amount of transplanted tissue is not excessive. After transplantation,the porcine cells can survive for several months and seem to be functional, even if the amounts of insulin produced are below normal (about 2 per cent of that of a healthy individual).

These attempts indicate that in the case of specific cells and tissues, pigs might be suitable as donors and to some extent are compatible with human physiology. Xenotransplants are increasingly being used in the effort to treat a wide variety of diseases such as Parkinson's disease and Huntington's disease, as well as epilepsy, and chronic intractable pain syndromes.

Organisation for Economic Co-operation and Development, *Xenotransplantation: International Policy Issues*, 1999.

"Altering the recipient's immune system before organ transplantation prevents the need for risky, long-term immunosuppressive therapy," Sykes says. "We believe that achieving a peaceful, harmonious coexistence between the immune cells of the donor and the recipient is the key to successful transplantation, whether within the same species or across species."

The technology is so promising, in fact, that Cosimi and Francis L. Delmonico, M.D., director of renal transplantation, have been given the green light to launch a pilot study using bone marrow transplantation to achieve tolerance in mismatched human-to-human kidney transplants. But such a clinical trial requires the identification of appropriate patients—which is no easy task.

"We are confident that we can achieve tolerance with this therapy," Sachs says. "Ethically, however, we don't want to deprive someone of standard immunosuppressive therapy, which we know works despite the potential long-term complications of powerful drugs, to offer a protocol that is untested in humans. The ideal candidate may be someone who needs a transplant but can't take the drugs necessary to suppress the immune system."

As surgeons stand at the brink of tolerance trials, investigations continue in the lively, fertile environment of the Transplantation Biology Research Center (TBRC). Focused on state-of-the-art animal care, the TBRC includes a fully equipped surgical suite and animal inpatient unit, featuring operating rooms, an isolation room, and an x-ray facility. Animals used in the laboratory receive the finest care and are treated humanely, Sachs says. Veterinarians specializing in the care of laboratory animals are with their charges constantly, checking, monitoring, providing round-the-clock nursing care, ensuring they are comfortable and well tended.

John Iacomini, Ph.D., a senior researcher in the TBRC, is studying gene therapy as a way to enhance tolerance. His group is extracting donor bone marrow and transforming its genetic makeup to make it more compatible with the recipient's marrow. "We have manipulated genes in mice, and others in the lab are doing similar work in large animals," Iacomini says. "This approach is hot. In fact, the TBRC laboratory of Christian LeGuern [Ph.D.] is the only place that has achieved tolerance in pigs using gene therapy."

Preventing Cross-Species Infections

In recent years, one of the most publicized concerns of cross-species transplants has been the risk of animal infections crossing over to humans. [In 1994,] Jay Fishman, M.D., of the Massachusetts General Infectious Disease Department, was talking with Sachs about xenotransplantation. Fishman asked what would happen when a pig organ was stitched into a human.

"David told me about rejection and how he planned to get around this barrier," Fishman says. "I said that was interesting, but I wanted to know what the organ would bring with it. Were there viruses or other pathogens that could be transplanted? That was the day I started working closely with David and his team."

Fishman, in fact, has become a well-recognized expert on these risks. [In fall 1996] he participated on the Food and Drug Administration and Institute of Medicine xenotransplantation panels. "The risk of transmission of infection from pig to human is real, but I believe it is small," Fishman now says. "We are—and will continue—taking every precaution to ensure that the donor animals are clean and free of known diseases."

Ensuring safety in xenotransplantation involves putting procedures into place for close and continuous monitoring and sampling of patients and animals. "We know we're at least several years away from clinical trials for xenotransplantation," Fishman says. "So we are taking advantage of this time to create probes to help monitor, detect, and manage any risks, including those posed by unknown viruses."

Fishman adds that one underpublicized benefit of xenotransplantation is that using the bone marrow or organs from swine could prevent infection associated with certain viruses. "We might be able to reconstitute bone marrow so that it is resistant to a human virus that destroyed the liver, for example," he says. "The patient who originally might not have been a candidate for a human organ transplant because of the presence of the virus, such as someone with hepatitis or AIDS, might be able to receive a pig organ because it might be resistant to viral infection."

Learning to Accept Animal Organs

To prepare for the time when clinical trials in xenotransplantation become reality, Massachusetts General Hospital [in 1996] convened a multidisciplinary committee representing all aspects of the technology—clinical, research, animal, ethical, and administrative. The committee drafted guidelines to inform and advise the hospital about the feasibility, logistics, safety, and social issues related to moving xenotransplantation from the laboratory to the bedside. The Xenotransplantation Advisory Committee also addressed various questions and concerns that could arise related to the technology.

One question that has been raised regarding xenotransplantation is the public's psychological willingness to accept transplanted organs from pigs. Cosimi says that some negative reaction is to be expected with such a nascent and unusual technology. He points out that many animal products, including cells and heart valves, for years have been placed into the human body. Widespread acceptance of xenotransplants, he says, will come about naturally when a good scientific model is in place and there exists a track record demonstrating that such transplants are safe and feasible.

"It's easy to say, 'I wouldn't accept a pig organ,' with no context and little understanding about the process," he says. "But let's face it: in the foxhole, everyone believes in God."

Cosimi says he can envision the day in the not-too-distant future when a patient comes to the hospital with acute liver failure, near death. "Instead of that desperate wait that too often proves futile, we can offer an organ right away. We can offer hope. And most important, we can save a life."

For the thousands of patients who desperately need an organ, and for their anxious families, that day cannot come soon enough.

| *"Although the medical risks of*
| *xenotransplantation are small in*
| *probability, they are of great magnitude."*

Xenotransplantation Is Dangerous

Mark J. Hanson

Xenotransplantation poses significant health risks and ethical problems, Mark J. Hanson maintains in the following viewpoint. He contends that transplanted animal organs could transmit diseases to human recipients, who in turn could infect other people. Hanson also argues that the recipients will have to learn how to cope with the knowledge that an important part of their bodies is nonhuman, in addition to facing physical burdens such as greater susceptibility to illnesses. The animals bred for organ transplantation will be negatively affected as well. Hanson is the executive director of the Missoula Demonstration Project, which was established to research the experience of dying persons and their families and demonstrate the effectiveness of community-based health care in improving the quality of life for the dying.

As you read, consider the following questions:
1. In Hanson's view, what are two problems with screening out transmissible diseases from source animals?
2. What is the most important question to ask before early clinical trials on xenotransplantation take place, according to Hanson?
3. According to the author, what animal welfare issues need to be considered when debating xenotransplantation?

Excerpted from "Xenotransplantation Protocol: Commentary," by Mark J. Hanson, *Hastings Center Report*, November 1999. Copyright © 1999 by The Hastings Center. Reprinted with permission.

Xenotransplantation raises a host of complex issues, challenging divisions between individual and public health, human and animal identity and welfare, and scientific progress and public concern about risk. Clearly, any technology that has the potential to ameliorate the very real suffering experienced by those waiting for organs should be explored, but given the uncertain circumstances the temptation actually to employ it should not be too quickly indulged.

The Threat of Zoonosis

The central question is whether xenotransplantation could transmit to humans a disease found in the animal—a zoonosis. While most transmissible diseases can be screened out of source animals, two problems remain. First, scientists can only screen for known pathogens, and there may be transmissible diseases that are yet undiscovered. Second, the consequences of infection by retroviruses from the source animals requires rigorous study. The effect of porcine retroviruses in human organ recipients over time is unpredictable and might not result in disease for many years, if ever. The risk may be extremely small, but the potential consequences of spawning a new pandemic are catastrophic.

Compounding the issue is the possibility that zoonoses could spread beyond the individual xenograft recipient to their intimates, to health care professionals, or even ultimately into the general population. Thus xenotransplantation represents a potential threat to the public health even if it provides a benefit to individual patients. Before clinical trials begin, therefore, scientific investigation of disease transmission risks must be as thorough as possible, with information made widely available.

The potential public health consequences of xenotransplantation complicate the moral obligation not to impose risk without the informed consent of those affected. The nature and degree of risk for disease transmission entail a moral obligation that consent be sought not only from the patient but also from his or her intimates and even—through some mechanism—from the general public itself. The ability for diseases to spread across borders makes xenotransplantation a truly global issue.

Complicating the issue of disease risk is uncertainty surrounding the assessment of that risk. Because the public health threats have not been demonstrated, the risks may appear "hypothetical" and thus not compelling in the face of medical benefit. But such reasoning is too easy; for the benefits of xenotransplantation, until they are demonstrated, are also hypothetical. Obligations to minimize risk entail that appropriate risk management strategies be implemented. On the local level, this includes case review by appropriately staffed institutional committees. Nationally, regulatory agencies should utilize such controls as protocol review bodies, patient registries, and tissue archives for humans and animals.

The Ethics of Xenotransplantation

As important as issues related to zoonoses are, however, a focus exclusively on disease risk reduces the breadth of considerations to essentially technical, scientific questions— answerable only by experts. Ethical consideration of a promising new medical technology often focuses on how most ethically to utilize it and overlooks broader questions about how it may subtly but significantly affect self-understanding and human relationships, or even about whether it is necessary at all. Xenotransplantation raises a variety of broader issues and risks that while vaguer and more difficult to evaluate are nevertheless important to consider.

The creation of transgenic animals [animals that have one or more heterologous genes incorporated in their chromosomes] and the placement of their organs and tissues within human beings transgresses boundaries long established and maintained by evolution. While human societies have long justified activities that are "unnatural" (such as medicine itself), it seems warranted, nevertheless, at least to probe how the "wisdom" of evolution may be challenged as technologies seek to blend species. Placing human genes in pigs and pig organs in human beings may not only be scientifically risky, it promotes subtle but not insignificant changes in world view and self-understanding.

More immediately, a xenograft recipient will have to bear significant physical and psychological burdens. At least the first generation of such patients should undergo a lifelong

The Spread of Deadly Viruses

Imagine a world where a previously unknown (and unrecognizable) virus is transmitted to a person through a transplanted animal organ, then races through the human population in a planetwide epidemic for which there is no cure.

A deadly virus transmitted to humans from animals is not science fiction. It has already happened. The 1918 influenza epidemic that killed more than 20,000,000 people worldwide was a mutated virus of swine flu evolved from American pigs and spread around the globe by U.S. troops mobilized for World War I. Humans already can acquire approximately 25 diseases from pigs, including anthrax, influenza, scabies, rabies, leptospirosis (which produces liver and kidney damage), and erysipelas (a skin infection). Researchers recently discovered that human tissue cells are susceptible to infection by pig retroviruses.

Alan H. Berger and Gil Lamont, *USA Today*, November 1999.

---

battery of regular medical tests and monitoring. They will likely be more prone to illness and may need to have their intimate relations restricted to minimize risk of disease transmission. Intimates may have to be monitored as well. Patients will also face the psychological issues attendant on such restrictions, in addition to the knowledge that a vital part of their own self is nonhuman, a fact that will likely not escape those bent on creating public sensation. Patients' relationships will most certainly be tested. Is the patient informed about these burdens and able and willing to undertake them? Will the patient be compliant, and what are the consequences of the inevitable noncompliant population in follow-up care? And all this raises what is perhaps the most important question to ask before beginning early clinical trials: What will count as success?

The Effects on Humans and Animals

Effects on the transplant and health care system in general should also be considered. Will fewer human organs and tissues be available? Are these medical resources being distributed justly? Who bears the financial and other burdens? Does xenotransplantation diminish health and cost lives by diverting resources from other areas of the health care system?

In addition, the risks and burdens incurred by xenotransplantation entail another test of trust between the public and physicians, government, and the biotechnology industry. Failure adequately to inform, obtain consent from, and protect patients and the public puts at risk public acceptance of future technologies that may provide real benefit.

Finally, the effects of transplantation ramify beyond the human community: animal welfare issues are also at stake. Source animals must be bred and maintained to become "pathogen free," which requires maintaining them in sterile and isolated environments. Genetic engineering to make their organs more compatible with human immune systems may affect their welfare. While medicine has long accepted the justifiability of using animals for medical purposes, the possibility of human benefit in itself does not justify all animal suffering. Welfare considerations are therefore relevant to the justifiability of xenotransplantation.

The considerable pressure to utilize new technologies into which millions of dollars have been invested is tremendous. But the real possibility of harms being imposed on patients and the public obligates all involved first to seek acceptable methods for avoiding those risks, medical and otherwise. This obligation entails a greater emphasis on prevention—that is, on finding ways to keep people from needing organs and tissues in the first place—and on developing alternative technologies. Use of split livers and living donors, changing human organ procurement strategies, developing stem cell technologies and artificial organs, and other perhaps less morally and medically problematic possibilities may render moot the question whether we want to incur the burdens imposed by xenotransplantation.

Although the medical risks of xenotransplantation are small in probability, they are of great magnitude. And much more is at stake than medical risks. Xenotransplantation should therefore be undertaken cautiously and only as a last resort.

> "*Even the most sophisticated treatments can't turn back the clock for aging eggs.*"

Fertility Treatments for Older Women Can Be Problematic

Sarah Scott

In the following viewpoint, Sarah Scott claims that despite reputed medical advances, women who seek to become pregnant after they turn forty experience many complications. According to Scott, egg quality declines as women reach their late thirties, thereby rendering reproductive technologies such as fertility drugs and in-vitro fertilizations largely ineffective. In addition, Scott contends that pregnancies that do occur are more likely to result in miscarriages and physical problems for the baby and mother when compared to the pregnancies of younger women. Scott is a writer for *Chatelaine*, a Canadian women's magazine.

As you read, consider the following questions:
1. What happens to the uterine lining as women age, according to Scott?
2. As stated by the author, what percentage of in-vitro fertilizations results in live births?
3. According to Scott, what are the effects of a high follicle-stimulating hormone level?

Y ou've seen the pictures of 40-ish celebrities proudly holding new babies. You've read about high-tech fertility miracles. Maybe you've heard the statistics on mature moms: the number of Canadian women giving birth after age 39 has more than doubled since 1985. So if you work out, don't smoke and look younger than your 40 years, you should be able to have a baby too, right? Think again. Despite the hype, medicine—even the most expensive high technology—can't necessarily deliver a baby.

Egg Quality Declines

At any age, getting pregnant is never guaranteed. Even if you time intercourse for your fertile days, healthy women under 35 have a 20 percent chance each month of conceiving a healthy baby. Five years later, your chances plummet to 5 percent. "Women have been duped into thinking you can delay," said Dr. Ruth Fretts, a Canadian obstetrician who teaches at Harvard Medical School. "Age matters."

It's mainly because of the eggs. You have 300,000 when you are born, but your stock declines throughout life. More important, the quality of the eggs declines in your late 30s, which significantly increases the risk of chromosomal abnormalities such as Down's syndrome. Older eggs don't function as well every step of the way—from fertilization to implantation—which explains why 40-plus women miscarry nearly three times more frequently than women who are 10 years younger.

Another less serious roadblock is the quality of the uterine lining, says Dr. Arthur Leader, chief of reproductive medicine at the University of Ottawa. As you approach menopause, you produce less of the hormone progesterone, so the lining of the uterus may not thicken enough to permit the fertilized egg to grow. Fortunately, progesterone levels can be topped up, either by injection or vaginal suppositories.

Limits of Technology

Even the most sophisticated treatments can't turn back the clock for aging eggs. Fertility drugs, for instance, might help regulate a woman's ovulation if her problems don't relate to menopause. But many reproductive specialists doubt the utility or ethics of using fertility drugs to pump out more 40-year-old eggs of poor quality. What's more, these treatments can cause side effects ranging from pelvic discomfort to double vision or hyperstimulation of the ovaries, which can result in metabolic problems or even internal bleeding. Fertility drugs might also increase the risk of ovarian cancer.

"QUICK, WHAT DO WE DO, DOC?...HER HIP BROKE THE SAME TIME HER WATER BROKE...!!"

Schorr. © 1997 by United Feature Syndicate. Reprinted with permission.

In-vitro fertilization (IVF) offers no baby-back guarantee either. Indeed, a U.S. survey charted 8,159 monthly cycles of assisted reproductive therapy, mainly in-vitro fertilization procedure. Women over age 40 took powerful fertility drugs to pump out as many eggs as possible, which were then combined with sperm in the laboratory and returned to their wombs. For couples trying to conceive by IVF, a live birth resulted only a disappointing 8 percent of the time. Now self-regulating Canadian IVF programs have all agreed to create a national registry and supply patients with their success rates so patients (many of whom are paying out of their own pockets) will have a better idea of their chances of conceiving.

If you're thinking about going the IVF route, which typically costs $7,000 per cycle, you might want to consider having a FSH (or follicle-stimulating hormone) test, which can predict your ability to conceive. As you get older, your unreleased eggs do not respond as well to normal levels of FSH. In an attempt to compensate and make the ovaries generate those eggs you have left, your body produces more FSH than it did when you were younger. So if your FSH level is high, it is likely that your reproductive clock is winding down and you will probably not respond very well to fertility treatment.

Newer Techniques

Modern medicine offers one effective solution: use a younger woman's eggs. The U.S. survey showed older women's chances of having a healthy baby jumped to 36.7 percent for each transfer of embryos made from donated eggs fertilized in vitro. But the idea makes many Canadians uncomfortable, so few clinics offer the procedure. At Toronto's IVF Canada, the waiting list for anonymous donor eggs is a year long. To bypass that wait, you could ask a sister or friend to donate. But donation involves taking fertility drugs and undergoing an uncomfortable procedure to retrieve the eggs.

Reproductive technology is getting closer to helping overcome the aging-egg factor by experimenting with some yet-unproven techniques. Drilling holes in shells of in-vitro embryos—since older eggs can have thicker shells—may help them "hatch" once they are implanted in the womb. Some IVF clinics now grow embryos in laboratory cultures for five days instead of two in order to weed out the ones that would have otherwise died. In the U.S., futuristic techniques such as injecting older eggs with cytoplasm or gel from younger eggs have produced a couple of babies.

Still, age is relative. Some women's biological clocks wind down more slowly than others', suggests a 1998 study coauthored by obstetrician Fretts. Among women who lived to age 100, a stunning 20 percent had given birth in their 40s. And that was long before test-tube babies.

*"Late motherhood provided just as much
love and devotion and in some respects was
more advantageous."*

Fertility Treatments for Older Women Should Not Be Discouraged

Roger Gosden

Fertility treatments, in particular in-vitro fertilization, have made it possible for women in their forties and fifties to become pregnant. In the following viewpoint, Roger Gosden contends that these pregnancies are less risky than critics claim and that late-in-life motherhood can be a positive experience for both mother and child. According to Gosden, older women experience few complications during their pregnancies, and their children do as well or better than the children of younger mothers. Gosden is a professor of reproductive biology at Leeds University in Leeds, England, and the author of *Designing Babies: The Brave New World of Reproductive Technology*, from which this excerpt was taken.

As you read, consider the following questions:

1. According to Gosden, what were some of the medical concerns cited by the National Institutes of Health in their study of late motherhood?
2. According to the survey conducted by Julia Berryman, what proportion of first-time mothers over the age of thirty-five would recommend the experience?
3. In Gosden's view, why are children of older parents more independent?

Excerpted from *Designing Babies: The Brave New World of Reproductive Technology*, by Roger Gosden (New York: W.H. Freeman, 1999). Copyright © 1999 by Roger Gosden. Reprinted with permission.

Our attitudes to those who choose to remain childless until mid-life tend to be ambivalent. People who have not enjoyed professional success may feel that no one should expect to "have it all." And to many it seems foolish or just plain selfish for a woman to begin a family in or after her late thirties. The older a woman is the more firmly these convictions are held, and a woman in her fifties trying to cross back over the menopausal Rubicon with the helping hand of science can expect almost universal condemnation. Needless to say, when a man of the same age fathers a child with a younger woman he wears his achievement with pride and is heartily congratulated. He only has to bear, at most, jokes in poor taste about the virtues of Viagra and the hazards of cuckoldry. . . .

A Questionable List of Problems

A meeting of fertility experts convened in 1998 at the National Institutes of Health to discuss medical concerns and to set research agendas for the American "epidemic" of late motherhood. We were told that cesarean sections, pregnancy diabetes, excess weight, and hypertension were all many times more likely in mothers of mature years. Also more babies were born too small or too large or too premature. According to the medical pessimists, a mother over 35 is a high-risk patient, and over-45 is a disaster waiting to happen. We were told that rather than expressing joy at the news of a positive pregnancy test, a doctor's reaction may be to darkly hint at termination even before prenatal screening has been done for the "sake of the health of the mother."

This list of despair should be taken with a pinch of salt, for medical minds are trained in averages but diseases and medical disasters occur as probabilities. Everyone is different, and our health and vigor decline with age at very different rates. Some people develop early the problems of old age, such as diabetes, heart disease, and bone loss, whereas luckier ones stay fit well into their seventies and eighties. It would be surprising if fertility were any different. Some people have the "change" at 45 and others at 55, some are fitter at 50 for pregnancy than others are at 30, although we put up obstacles only for the first.

People should always be treated as individuals whatever their age, and those who are fit enough ought to be given the green light for fertility treatment. When Mark Sauer, then at the University of Southern California, provided egg donation for superfit women between 40 and 52, he provoked fury, even though the pregnancies turned out to be successful and had few complications. Nowadays, treatment of this age group in American in-vitro fertilization [IVF] units no longer draws so much comment. The age of contention has risen to 60, and the world record for delivery now stands at 63. Some people weather better than others, and there is a connection between reproductive fitness and all-around health. Those who have had a late baby naturally or a late menopause are more likely to live longer and join the salon of centenarians. Since lives have become healthier and longer, a woman giving birth even at 60 can expect as many years with her child as her grandmother had with her last one.

Older Mothers Have Positive Experiences

The quality of those years count more than the quantity, but few people have taken the trouble to discover the experiences of older mothers. Julia Berryman, a psychologist at Leicester University, has conducted a rare survey of hundreds of women contacted through appeals in newspapers and women's magazines. A group of women aged over 35 at their first delivery was compared with a group of women of the same social class who were in their twenties at the time of first delivery. The results were reassuring. Most of the older women were "very happy" and nine out of ten recommended the experience. Pregnancy was no more bothersome, though there were the usual irritations—heartburn, swollen feet and ankles, unruly bladders, and aching backs—and the older women were more likely to suffer extreme tiredness (although not all do). Despite few complications, more were signed up for cesarean sections by doctors who were skeptical that their uterine muscle had enough athletic prowess to manage labor. Fewer older mothers declared that they had bonded with the baby by mid-pregnancy, perhaps because they had miscarried in the past and they regarded pregnancy as a more uncertain condition or perhaps because they were worried about having a fetus with Down's syndrome, a worry that would have been reinforced by the greater attention on pregnancy screening.

Not a Popular Option

Post-retirement babies are not going to be a popular option, for either sex, any time soon. Most people in their 60s with the necessary cash, leisure and vigor have other plans—playing the slots, driving around the country in R.V.s, writing angry letters to their representatives about attempts to recalculate the consumer price index. If every now and then a woman feels driven to put herself through gynecological hell . . . why can't we just add it to the very long list of oddball things people do and leave the whole Miracle Family [referring to a sixty-three-year-old woman who gave birth in spring 1997] alone?

Katha Pollitt, *Nation*, May 26, 1997.

Most parents put above all else the interests of their babies, who need more than a healthy womb and a full breast to get a good start in life. The Leicester survey found that late motherhood provided just as much love and devotion and in some respects was more advantageous. The older mothers had more positive attitudes to discipline, resorting to physical punishment less frequently in the training of their children, and they made more earnest attempts to breast-feed. The children were encouraged to be more independent, perhaps because the mothers and fathers were more self-confident after years of working. Yet the infants were evidently not shortchanged, for they acquired higher scores in verbal skills by 4 years old, were more self-motivated, less easily distracted, and more intellectually advanced (though not necessarily more intelligent). Older fathers spent less time at play but were more likely to sit with their child reading stories or watching TV and reliving memories of the receding days of their own childhood.

Perhaps we should not be surprised that baby boomers are in earnest about giving their kid(s) a good start in life and preparing them for the competitive world ahead. Concerns about a bigger generation gap than in earlier decades are probably unwarranted and would be puzzling to many cultures. Children in West Africa and other parts of the world are traditionally raised by their grandparents. A break with custom always triggers anxiety, but, put into perspective, older families have slight impact on society compared with the steady dissolution of the traditional extended family, which is now far advanced in the West. Besides, the children of older parents are more likely to have all their needs (and more of their wants) met and, because these families tend to be smaller, are unlikely to suffer from want of attention.

A Minor Revolution

The edging up of maternal age is hardly perceptible from year to year, but with hindsight a minor revolution has occurred. Most American births are still to women in their twenties, but the average age for starting a family has crept up to 28, and 10% of births now occur after 35, with similar trends in Europe among the middle classes. The percentage of women aged 30 to 34 years having their first child rose from 7% to 22% between 1973 and 1994, and the increase was even higher for those aged 34 to 44. Many of the late maternities are to middle-class and better-educated couples. After the age of 40 more pregnancies now lead to delivery than termination, which says a lot about attitudes, and the women seem to be prouder of being an older parent and to care less about being mistaken for a grandmother collecting a child after school. When left to their own devices, people invest in reproduction according to what they perceive as their best interests.

"It's possible that human beings may die so that embryos will live."

Embryonic Stem Cell Research Will Save Lives

Richard Cohen

Scientists believe that stem cells can be controlled and used to replace diseased organs and tissues in the treatment of diseases such as Parkinson's and Alzheimer's. On August 9, 2001, President George W. Bush announced that he would allow research only on existing human embryonic stem cell lines, provided that the stem cells came from embryos that no longer had the possibility of developing as human beings. In the following viewpoint, Richard Cohen asserts that limiting embryonic stem cell research is unethical because these studies may help save the lives of many people. According to Cohen, President Bush's decision to restrict research on embryos—based on the position that embryos are human beings—disregards the laws of nature and could cost many people their lives. Cohen is an op-ed columnist for the *Washington Post*.

As you read, consider the following questions:
1. According to Cohen, what is one of the steps that must occur for a fertilized egg to become a life?
2. What does Hubert Markl mean by "biologism"?
3. In Cohen's opinion, how do pro-lifers attempt to overrule nature?

Through the miracle of modern science—miniaturization and all of that—this (viewpoint) will take you into the fallopian tubes of your ordinary woman of childbearing age. A sperm is swimming like crazy toward the egg. It makes contact and fertilizes it. The egg then moves up the tube so that it can attach itself to the wall of the womb. But—oh, no!—it cannot do so. No pregnancy results. Oh well, maybe next time.

The First Stage in the Process

This process takes place—okay, I have invented the statistic—2.6 billion times a month. That is the number of times sexual intercourse produces a fertilized egg that does not, for some reason, result in a pregnancy. If it were left to its own devices, nothing would happen. Still, is that fertilized egg a life? The answer is no. Life requires additional steps—adhering to the wall of the womb, just for starters. Life requires progressing from the embryo stage to the fetus stage—and maybe then some. But if the process is interrupted, which is more the rule than the exception in nature, then we do not have life. We had merely the potential for it.

And yet, it is at that very stage in the process—the mere production of a fertilized egg—that George W. Bush and his fellow "pro-lifers" declare that a "human being" has been created, a term Bush himself has used in reference to mere embryos, particularly those created by cloning. So the harvesting of these fertilized eggs, the embryos, cannot be permitted even though they might wind up saving the lives of people who now will die from one disease or another. How that can be called pro-life is beyond me.

Anyone can see that, ultimately, stem cell research and the related field of cloning are going to produce ethical questions galore. But the one that exists at the moment is entirely manufactured—the product of calling an embryo a "human being." Only by doing that do you get a dilemma, a supposed tradeoff between the "human being" residing in a petri dish that's the embryo and the "human being" that's an actual human being, residing maybe in your own home. It is interesting to pause here and ask why most embryos don't adhere to the uterine wall. Sometimes it's because the em-

Britt. © 2001 by Copley Media Services. Reprinted with permission.

bryos have genetic abnormalities. Sometimes, though, these abnormal embryos do not self-abort and when that is the case, a severely handicapped baby may result. In other words, by not interfering—by letting nature take its (mistaken) course—a heartbreaking tragedy can occur.

An Inhuman Determinism

I take this example from a speech given by Hubert Markl, the president of Germany's renowned Max Planck Society, which was reprinted in the scientific journal *Nature*. He uses the term "biologism" to refer to what really is the basis for Bush's thinking: Anything produced by human beings is human and cannot be trifled with.

Thus, we get stuck with a kind of awful determinism, embracing as "human" embryos that nature ordinarily rejects. The pro-lifers would even overrule nature itself, insisting that anything moving through the birth canal is a human being and thus inviolate. They know, somehow, that this is what God intended—even for some incomprehensible reason, the birth of a Tay-Sachs baby which will live in agony and die prematurely. [Tay-Sachs is a genetic disease that leads to a loss of sight and health functions.]

But as Markl points out, the ability to choose—to use our noggin—is the quintessentially human characteristic. And yet this gets rejected in favor of a determinism that is not human at all. It is merely chemistry in action. In the purported cause of forbidding others from playing God, Bush and like-minded people would themselves play God. As is usually the case, everyone seems to know what God intends.

In a way, the stem cell controversy is the absurd product of the fight against abortion. Who could have thought that back when most of us took sides, some of us would have wound up defending late-term abortions on the one hand while others would denounce stem cell research? In both cases, principle has thoroughly trashed common sense.

Common sense would at least suggest that we are entitled to do what nature itself does all the time. Yet, by fiat based on religious belief, the president has decided to severely limit stem cell research funded by the government and maybe even conducted by private industry as well. In the end, it's possible that human beings may die so that embryos will live. This is not an ethical dilemma. It is an ethical travesty.

"The entire purpose of the embryonic stem cell controversy has been to advance a new collectivist medical ethic."

Embryonic Stem Cell Research Could Have Dangerous Consequences

William Norman Grigg

Permitting research on embryonic stem cells is unnecessary and could lead to further violations of individual rights, William Norman Grigg claims in the following viewpoint. According to Grigg, President Bush's decision to permit research on existing stem cell lines could be used in the future to justify policies such as organ harvesting. Grigg argues that using adult stem cells instead of embryonic cells will enable research to continue without sacrificing the weaker members of society. Grigg is the senior editor of the magazine *New American*.

As you read, consider the following questions:
1. What George W. Bush expression does the author consider "Clintonesque"?
2. How many stem cell lines exist, according to the July 2001 study by the National Institutes of Health?
3. According to Grigg, what was Vladimir Lenin's key political question?

From "Medical Cannibalism," by William Norman Grigg, *New American*, September 20, 2001. Copyright © 2001 by American Opinion Publishing, Inc. Reprinted with permission.

The quotes you are about to read are true. The circumstances have been changed in order to illustrate the fatally flawed moral reasoning behind President Bush's unconstitutional decision to subsidize experimentation on existing "lines" of stem cells extracted from human embryos.

A Look into the Future

Washington, D.C., August 9, 2003: President George W. Bush announced today that he would allow federal funding for medical experiments using organs and tissues "harvested" from executed Chinese prisoners. In a live address to the nation, the President underscored the fact that he had invested four months of anguished reflection and prayer into the effort to reach this decision. One key consideration, the President observed, was the fact that since the bodies of the executed prisoners are "going to be destroyed anyway," the organs that have been extracted from them should "be used for a greater good, for research that has the potential to save and improve other lives. . . ." He also emphasized that the subsidies would be limited to the existing stock of "harvested" organs, "where the life and death decision has already been made." Because this medical research "offers both great promise and great peril," said Mr. Bush, "I have decided we must proceed with great care."

Referring to media reports that Red Chinese authorities had imprisoned some people "solely to experiment upon them," the President declared: "This is deeply troubling, and a warning sign that should prompt all of us to think through these issues very carefully. . . . We recoil at the idea of growing human beings for spare body parts, or creating life for our convenience."

One spokesman for the National Council of Catholic Bishops denounced the President's decision: "For the government to allow funding for this experiment makes the government complicit in what we consider to be wrongdoing." However, a spokesman for the United Methodist Church—the President's denomination—offered qualified approval for the decision, noting that "if you're going to do this research with federal funding, he narrowed it as much as he could." Similar ambivalent approval was given by Focus on the Family, a major "Christian Right" organization. "From our perspective he didn't call for federal funds to be expended to take human life," commented Focus on the Family President Dr. James Dobson. Although the group remains opposed to the use of organs harvested from Chinese prisoners, those who would be affected by the President's decision "are now gone," continued Dr. Dobson. Meanwhile, the harvested organs "are there and I think we can live with that."

Entering the Culture of Death

None of the people mentioned in this fictional example support the harvesting of organs from Chinese prisoners. Our descent into the Culture of Death has not yet reached such a critical stage. Nevertheless—and this is the point of our exercise in extrapolation—there is nothing in President Bush's [August 9, 2001] speech that would prevent us from getting there.

It's not difficult to recall how mainstream conservatives reacted to Bill Clinton's cagy equivocation [during the Monica Lewinsky scandal] about the meaning of the word "is." Many of those same conservatives have been curiously silent about George W. Bush's Clintonesque use of the expression "potential for life" to describe the status of the human embryos from which stem cells are cannibalized. If human embryos merely represent "potential" life, what is so scandalous about creating them "solely to experiment upon them"? But then again, Bush did not say that creating a human life—or "potential" life—for that purpose should be forbidden, but merely that it is something we should "think through . . . very carefully."

In announcing that he was limiting federal subsidies to the "more than 60 genetically diverse stem cell lines" that already exist, Bush may actually have issued a mandate for further killing. A July [2001] study by the National Institutes of Health (NIH) on stem cell research declared: "At the time of this report, there are approximately 30 cell lines of human pluripotent stem cells that have been derived from human blastocysts or fetal tissue." Assuming Bush offered an accu-

The Benefits of Adult Stem Cells

Even without federal funds, nay even without embryonic cells, stem-cell research has made tremendous strides toward bringing hope to persons with . . . [diseases such as Alzheimer's and heart disease] along with many others. . . .

Why aren't we hearing about this? Simple: It's scientific ignorance, with a dollop of disinformation tossed in for good measure. Advances in tissue-regeneration research are coming fast and furious because of something either ignored or pooh-poohed by embryonic-cell advocates—non-embryonic stem cells. Scientists are finding such stem cells in tissues throughout the body, then converting them into an incredible array of mature cells with the ability to combat a vast number of devastating diseases and injuries.

Yet across the board, proponents of lifting the embryonic-cell research ban either are ignorant or pretend to be ignorant of the tremendous advances in non-embryonic stem-cell research.

Michael Fumento, *National Review*, July 23, 2001.

---

rate figure, where did the other 30 stem cell lines come from? Was he authorizing the creation of additional lines beyond those that presently exist? And what is the origin of the "fetal tissue" referred to by the NIH?

A New Medical Ethic

Bush noted that fetal tissue research "has not lived up to its expectations." What he avoided mentioning is that there is no scientific justification for using embryonic rather than "adult" stem cells in medical research—and that adult stem cells can be obtained without killing a developing human individual.

But the entire purpose of the embryonic stem cell controversy has been to advance a new collectivist medical ethic in which the rights of the individual can be violated in the name of society's greater good. Under the same principle, handicapped or elderly adults (or Chinese prisoners, for that matter) could someday be forced to serve as organ or tissue donors—once again, in the name of the collective good of society.

For Vladimir Lenin [the founder of Bolshevism and

leader of the Soviet government following the 1917 Russian Revolution], the key question of politics was "Kto kogo"— "Who consumes whom?" By extending federal subsidy to a form of medical cannibalism in the name of the "greater good," Bush endorsed the application of Lenin's political ethics to medicine.

Periodical Bibliography

The following articles have been selected to supplement the diverse views presented in this chapter.

Alan H. Berger and Gil Lamont — "Animal Organs Won't Solve the Transplant Shortage," *USA Today*, November 1999.

Richard Cohen — "An Ethical Travesty," *Washington Post*, August 14, 2001.

Theodore Dalrymple — "Families to Go," *Spectator*, January 2000.

Sharon Driedger — "Racing the Biological Clock," *Maclean's*, January 26, 1998.

Cynthia Fox — "Why Stem Cells Will Transform Medicine," *Fortune*, June 11, 2001.

John J. Fung — "Transplanting Animal Organs into Humans Is Feasible," *USA Today*, November 1999.

Robert P. George — "Don't Destroy Human Life," *Wall Street Journal*, July 30, 2001.

Roger Gosden — "New Options for Mothers," *Futurist*, March 2000.

Scott Gottlieb — "Adult Cells Do It Better," *American Spectator*, June 5, 2001.

Stephen S. Hall — "Adult Stem Cells," *Technology Review*, November 2001.

Ian Hutchinson — "The Ethics of Xenotransplantation," *Biological Sciences Review*, November 1999.

Claudia Kalb — "How Old Is Too Old?" *Newsweek*, May 5, 1997.

M. Therese Lysaught — "Holy Grail or Pandora's Box?" *World & I*, November 1999.

Katha Pollitt — "When I'm Sixty-Four," *Nation*, May 26, 1997.

Nicholas Wade — "Grappling with the Ethics of Stem Cell Research," *New York Times*, July 24, 2001.

CHAPTER 4

What Is the Future of Medicine?

Chapter Preface

Gene therapy is an emerging medical procedure in which normal or genetically altered genes are inserted into patients' cells in the hopes of curing cancer, heart disease, or numerous genetic ailments. The first gene therapy clinical trial was held in 1989; since that time, the National Institutes of Health (NIH) has conducted more than five hundred trials, involving over four thousand people. Unfortunately, not all gene therapy trials have gone well, and the problems have raised questions about the safety of gene therapy.

On September 17, 1999, eighteen-year-old Jesse Gelsinger died during a gene therapy experiment. He had been participating in a test for a potential treatment for ornithine transcarbamylase (OTC) deficiency, a metabolic disorder that keeps the liver from breaking down ammonia. The adenovirus—a virus that causes respiratory diseases—that was used to deliver the genetic material into Gelsinger's body caused his immune system to overreact. Within the next four days, Gelsinger suffered from systemic blood clotting, respiratory disease, and liver and kidney failure before he finally died.

Gelsinger's death has led to a call for more stringent monitoring of gene therapy research and clinical trials. The Food and Drug Administration (FDA) and NIH are responsible for ensuring that these trials are regulated and safely conducted. In February 2000, officials from the FDA and NIH were among those who testified at a congressional hearing on the safety of gene therapy; Gelsinger's father and genetics experts also gave testimony. Amy Patterson, who is a director at the NIH, reported during the hearing that 652 adverse events had occurred during seven years of studies. However, according to Patterson, the NIH had not learned about many of these incidents until after November 1999, when it urged federally funded researchers to report any adverse events. Other steps that have been taken by the FDA and NIH to promote the safety of gene therapy clinical trials is to mandate that all researchers provide patient records and study protocols to the appropriate regulatory agencies and to list all trials at the government website http://clinicaltrials.gov so patients can learn about the trials and any potential adverse effects of the treatments.

Despite the call for restrictions on gene therapy clinical trials, many people argue that gene therapy could be beneficial and that further research should not be hindered. Such therapy has already shown promise in treating cystic fibrosis, head and neck cancer, and muscular dystrophy. Ellen Licking, a writer for *Business Week*, contends, "It would be unfortunate if the criticism leads to unnecessary delays in gene therapy research. Scientists are barely a decade into the research, and one of the most important things they've discovered so far is that perfecting the techniques will be more difficult than they had hoped."

Gene therapy will likely play an important part in the future of medicine. In the following chapter, the authors examine the treatments and policies that could change medicine in the coming years.

*"A genetically driven medical renaissance . . .
has already begun to advance our potential
in health care."*

Genetic Cures Will Cause a Medical Renaissance

G. Terry Sharrer

In the following viewpoint, G. Terry Sharrer asserts that discoveries by geneticists, such as the identification of individual variations within human genes, will lead to a medical renaissance. According to Sharrer, a greater understanding of human genetics will lead to medical advances such as "chimeraplasty," a technique used to repair the defective genes that cause disease. Sharrer contends that "gene medicine" will extend life expectancy and improve the quality of life for many patients. Sharrer is the curator of health sciences at the Smithsonian Institution in the District of Columbia and a board member of the National Foundation for Cancer Research.

As you read, consider the following questions:

1. According to Sharrer, what will likely be the future purpose of microarray machines?
2. What does the author believe will result from microscale diagnostics?
3. What was the effect of chimeraplasty on rats with Crigler-Najjar syndrome, according to the author?

Color, rubor, dolor, tumor (heat, redness, pain, and swelling)—the cardinal signs of inflammation that [Roman medical writer] Aulus Cornelius Celsus taught in the first century A.D.—provided a focus for medicine that continued through the next two millennia. Over time, physicians sorted out diseases, developed diagnostics, and found effective remedies, but proficiency in healing was largely related to overcoming symptoms. Medicine's future, however, holds a new dimension, one dealing with the origins of disease—more precisely, specific versions of particular disorders, which may vary from individual to individual.

Genetics and Diseases

The energizer for this new approach has been the Human Genome Project's[1] attempts to discover not only all the genes of our species but even the "single-nucleotide polymorphisms" (SNPs) that distinguish one person's genome from another's. With the discovery that many diseases arise from genetic defects, public attention has converged on the associated genes. But SNPs have drawn less notice, partly because their role in illnesses is not entirely clear.

SNPs are variations in the individual units (nucleotides) of the overall DNA structure. They occur about once in every 1,000 nucleotides of sequence, which means that there are conceivably 3 million SNPs in the human genome. Not even identical twins have identical SNPs. Most of these variations are in "noncoding regions," where the DNA sequence carries no instructions for protein synthesis. But some appear to be distantly linked to functional genes, and others are located within functional genes, where they may or may not exert a detectable influence. An example of an SNP with functional consequence would be a point mutation in a gene that leads to a disease.

The genetics of colon cancer illustrates this specificity. About 95 percent of colon cancer patients have an adenocarcinoma (a type of tumor) in the colon, and nearly all of

---

1. The Human Genome Project, which began in 1990, is a thirteen-year effort to identify the approximately 30,000 genes in human DNA and determine the sequences of the DNA's 3 billion chemical base pairs.

them have mutated genes on at least chromosomes 3, 5, 12, 17, and 18. These mutations began accumulating in a single cell that started the abnormal growth. Within each of those genes, however, hundreds of different point mutations are possible, causing functional changes. Each patient's repertoire of point mutations is distinct if not unique, leading to the inference that there may be nearly as many forms of colon cancer as there are people with that disease.

For diseases such as cystic fibrosis (CF), where the disorder is linked to a single defective gene, there is a mutation in the same nucleotide in many cases, but not in others. As a result, there is considerable diversity among those who ail from the same CF symptoms. Furthermore, SNPs have been implicated in such areas as susceptibility to infections, reaction to drugs, and even daily nutritional requirements.

It's ambitious to assume that all diseases can be subdivided into small groups, down to even individual expressions. In the nineteenth century, germ theory did something similar: It classified pyrexias (fevers) according to different causative pathogens. But will a medical approach that repairs genes ever be customized for individual patients? So far, expectations have outpaced results.

Improvements in Diagnostics

The surge in expectations is buttressed by remarkable innovations in diagnostics. Researchers have already developed microarray machines in which thousands of discrete DNA sequences are attached to glass chips. In the foreseeable future, the entire human genome might be represented on a single chip. The strategy is that DNA fragments would be isolated from an individual, tagged with a fluorescent label, and tested for specific binding (hybridization) to complementary sequences on the chips. Each person's DNA sequence would produce a characteristic binding pattern, detectable by an optical scanner.

Analysis of gene sequences would be followed by analysis of gene expression—that is, the production of specific types of RNA and proteins. It should then become possible to understand a patient's changing biochemistry in much finer detail than is possible today. Miniaturization of instruments used in biological analysis could bring the technology that's currently available only in major research hospitals to the local clinic or private doctor's office. And it is not far-fetched to imagine an annual "checkup" involving the comparison of a recent microarray analysis with an earlier evaluation recorded on a CD-ROM.

Peters. © 2000 by Daytona Daily News. Reprinted by permission of Tribune Media Services.

It now appears that an individual's SNPs may determine how much of a drug remains in his body over time, as well the extent of benefits and likely side effects of the drug. From that perspective, microscale diagnostics might lead to better medicines, new indications for older drugs, and a decline in the 100,000 annual deaths (in the United States) caused by adverse reactions.

New Purposes for Gene Therapy

The original concept of gene therapy—to replace a defective gene with a properly functioning one—has barely met with proof on the practical level. Since the beginnings of this therapy in September 1990, some 300 clinical trials involving about 6,000 patients have been conducted, but the results have been mostly disappointing. Nonetheless, if gene-replacement therapy is geared to the individual's genetic makeup, it may eventually become an adjuvant to chemotherapy and radiation, lessening their severity or enhancing their effectiveness.

Meanwhile, scientists at Kimeragen (in Newtown, Pennsylvania) have devised a newer strategy—termed *chimeraplasty*—to repair defective genes. [Kimeragen Inc. merged with the French company ValiGene to form ValiGen.] Whereas gene therapy mainly uses genetically engineered viruses to deliver a replacement gene, chimeraplasty relies on short, synthetically produced sequences of DNA/RNA hybrids (chimeraplasts) to interact with the faulty genetic material and to stimulate the cell's genetic repair mechanism to correct the defects.

The first clinical protocol, tested on rats, was designed to treat Crigler-Najjar syndrome—a genetic disease in which a defective liver enzyme fails to break down bilirubin, which at high levels can damage the central nervous system. The chimeraplasts were cleverly introduced into the nuclei of liver cells, where the chimeraplasts' sequence matched almost perfectly with a complementary sequence on a chromosome. But a mismatch of one nucleotide, at the point mutation linked to the disease, activated the cellular DNA repair enzymes to fix the defective gene. Widening the applications for this approach would mainly depend on finding the delivery systems for specific types of cells.

If this type of "gene medicine" delivers on its promise, the individual diagnosis and treatment of disease holds many startling eventualities. Intractable, chronic diseases—such as cancer, stroke, Alzheimer's, and diabetes—might be beaten down. This approach may extend life expectancy a little further, but more important, it would tremendously improve the quality of life for those who would otherwise suffer.

Of course, at present it is almost unimaginable that a drug company might someday customize its medicines to suit each patient, or that an insurance company would pay for that. But where there's a way, there may be a will. Diseases will never disappear from the human condition, but a genetically driven medical renaissance—or "genaissance," to borrow the name of one company working in this rising field—has already begun to advance our potential in health care.

"*It isn't just that gene therapy for rare disorders doesn't pay. [Biotechnology companies] can't get it to work even when money is no object.*"

The Promise of Genetic Cures Has Been Exaggerated

Tom Bethell

In the following viewpoint, Tom Bethell claims that scientific and mainstream media are overstating the benefits of gene therapy. He asserts that despite the claims of many articles, little is known about the human genome. Bethell also maintains that gene therapy will likely not cure either heritable or nonheritable diseases and that the beneficiaries of genome discoveries will be biotechnology companies, not patients. Bethell is the senior editor of the *American Spectator*.

As you read, consider the following questions:
1. According to estimates cited by Bethell, what is the number of human genes?
2. Why does gene therapy fail to cure diseases such as sickle cell anemia and muscular dystrophy, as stated by Bethell?
3. What does the author claim is the "permanent tendency of medical science"?

From "Boastful Genome Science," by Tom Bethell, *American Spectator*, September 2000. Copyright © 2000 by *American Spectator*. Reprinted with permission.

Journalists . . . reserve the right to question national security policy, the CIA, defense issues, tax cuts, and so on. It's a good thing they do, too (not that they do it enough). But when it comes to science, the adversary press is a no-show.

With the [human] genome project [an effort to determine the sequences of human DNA's 3 billion chemical base pairs and identify the approximately 30,000 genes in human DNA,] the *New York Times*, the *Washington Post*, and indeed *Science* magazine managed to present the scientific claims at two levels. At the front-page, propaganda level, the Heroic Deeds of Science were presented uncritically. They are state-approved, the bandwagon is rolling, and the reporters know they are not expected to raise doubts. . . . Network television exists solely at this level.

Understanding Science Reporting

On the inside pages, however, you could find facts that undermined the headlines. But few readers ever get to the fine print, and that is the way science reporting works. The publicity ensures that the flow of public funds continues; Congress is reassured that "the people" support this bold initiative. It's something like the *Pravda* [the official newspaper of the Soviet Union] of old, with stale propaganda in the headlines, and, sometimes, useful information popping up inside.

The "inside" accounts, plus a little checking I did on my own, make me wonder whether the genome project amounts to much, so far. A few illustrations: An oped in the *New York Times* by David Baltimore, the president of Caltech, was headlined "50,000 Genes, and We Know Them All (Almost)." A few days earlier, the July 2000 *Scientific American* appeared. One story said: "Now that all the 100,000 or so genes that make up the human genome have been deciphered. . . ." At the Cold Spring Harbor Laboratory, they were making bets on the final number of human genes. Estimates ranged from 27,462 to 200,000. Why did the range increase even as more and more of the genome was "decoded"? Rick Weiss of the *Washington Post* said the problem is that "it can be difficult to tell where a gene begins and ends in the three billion letter sequence of human genetic code."

Yet Baltimore had begun his article: "Humans have no

more genetic secrets; our genes are a book open to all to read." He knew that wasn't true, of course. Here he was in the approved Bandwagon mode. (And if Nobel Prize winners can do it, why not humble journalists?) A couple of days later the same Baltimore was quoted in the *New York Times* as saying: "Complexity is the word on everybody's lips these days when they see what the genome really looks like. We've got another century of work ahead of us, to figure out how all of these things relate to each other." No more genetic secrets, then, and a century will be needed to figure things out.

I phoned a scientist with two years experience at the genome institute headed by Francis Collins. (It is one of the 25 divisions of the National Institutes of Health.) Why was everyone so hazy about the number of genes, I asked. Off the record, he was candid. He wasn't sure of the answer himself! Which told me what I had suspected—that that the genome people are much closer to the beginning of this project than they are to the end. Baltimore may well be right when he says that it may take another 100 years.

The gene today is thought of as a compromise between the classical "factor" of Mendelian genetics (a hypothetical construct, invisible yet controlling an outward trait of the organism) and the DNA molecule of Watson and Crick. Genes are said to be specific segments of the 3.15 billion-unit chain of DNA, and each gene is said to "code for" one protein. But now it seems there are far more proteins than there are genes. So the whole notion of the gene is conceptually a mess right now, and it may be that the recent (post-DNA) understanding of it will have to be discarded. I won't even get into the 97 percent of the genome whose function is not known. Scientists still sometimes call it "junk," but I was glad to see Dr. Collins cautioning against that hubris.

Here's a misconception encouraged by eager-beaver scientists and their press agents. The *New York Times* had this big front-page headline: "Genetic Code of Human Life Is Cracked by Scientists." Code cracked. Code decoded. That has been the message. But the "code" has, precisely, not been cracked. It would be more true to say that the DNA has been put into code—encoded. We have a string of nucleotides in sequence (A's, C's, G's, and T's), but to a very large extent we don't know what these sequences are doing. They are still in code.

Curing Profitable Diseases

You may ask, what about the private sector? What about the 2,500-odd biotech companies around the U.S., perhaps 80 percent of them hoping to use genome data to cook up something they can sell. Doesn't this show that, government hype notwithstanding, a real payoff is coming down the road? This is where it gets interesting, and where the fine print becomes crucial. Meanwhile, bear in mind that for the investment-hungry, sizzle-selling biotechs, a publicity bonanza is even more important than it is for the government.

Gene Therapy Experiments Are Misdirected

According to Abbey S. Meyers, "the great majority of gene therapy experiments are not conducted on genetic diseases, which are too rare to encourage investment capital, but on cancer, primarily because investors sense that a potential treatment for cancer will be more profitable." This is unfortunate, because genetic diseases—those which involve the absence or mutation of a single or very few genes with little or no environmental influence—clearly offer the most promise of success for this fledgling therapy. Cancer, on the other hand, is an extremely complex disease process that involves multiple genes as well as many environmental factors. Gene therapy experimentation on cancer patients might be compared to the misplaced ambition of a rookie ball player who strikes out every time at bat by attempting to hit home runs rather than slowly honing his skills by swinging for base hits. The home runs will come in time. For now, this misdirected focus probably helps explain the utter failure of gene therapy to achieve any confirmed cures after 10 years of experimentation on thousands of patients.

Bill Freese, written testimony, Subcommittee on Public Health, February 2, 2000.

Compare, again, the headlines and the buried story. On page one we often saw something like this: "Understanding the human genome is expected to revolutionize the practice of medicine." Here is a contrasting comment buried inside the *New York Times* [in 1998]:

The focus of gene therapy has shifted from inherited diseases toward more common ailments like cancer, AIDS and heart disease—all areas that could prove more profitable. Many genetic diseases, and there are thousands of them, affect anywhere from a handful to a few thousand people worldwide, hardly a commercial prospect for pharmaceutical companies. "The whole concept of gene therapy for genetic diseases doesn't fit the business model," said Dr. James M. Wilson, director of the institute for human gene therapy at the University of Pennsylvania and president of the American Society for Gene Therapy.

That is still true today.

It isn't just that gene therapy for rare disorders doesn't pay. They can't get it to work even when money is no object. And they have been trying for years.

Fine print: "'We've had our gene since 1989, says Dr. Robert Beall, president of the Cystic Fibrosis Foundation. Despite high hopes for a gene therapy that would repair the lung tissues of the 30,000 cystic fibrosis sufferers, none has emerged." (*Wall Street Journal*, June 26, 2000) The point mutations that cause muscular dystrophy, Huntington's chorea, Tay-Sachs disease, and sickle cell anemia have also been known, in some cases for decades. But they cannot now be cured by gene therapy. The reason is that the mutation is in the germ line, which means that the defect appears in every cell in the body. It is impossible to get the repaired gene into enough cells to make a difference. As for infusing the body with the essential protein that the defective gene cannot make, that can't be done either because the biochemistry of proteins is still not well enough understood.

The Likely Results of Gene Therapy

The result is that scientists are now to a large extent looking for disease-causing mutations that arise not in the germ line but in the course of ordinary cell division. But here they have a very different problem. They have not yet shown that these "somatic" mutations (as they are called) cause any disease at all. Mostly, they are looking for cancer-causing genes. Of the 420-odd gene therapy experiments approved by the Recombinant DNA Advisory Committee at the NIH since 1989, about 220 have involved the hunt for cancer genes, while 30 have tested ever more complex theories about HIV. My belief is that none of these experiments will work out. The awesome possibility exists that gene therapy won't work with mutations that give rise to heritable diseases, and they won't work either with non-heritable mutations, because they don't cause diseases!

At the moment, the genome discoveries will mainly generate diagnostic tests. . . . With their vaunted diagnostics, doctors will be telling more and more patients they are "at risk" for this and that. And an arsenal of risky drugs will be prescribed, some of them no doubt best avoided (but most patients will be too intimidated to say no). One sad result of genetic testing is that "therapeutic" abortions will increasingly be advocated. Already, some women are getting their breasts removed because they are said to harbor tumor-causing genes (although they are not present in the majority of breast cancers).

So biotechs will probably do a brisk business in diagnostic devices. Mostly they sell goods to one another, or to the big drug companies. Some biotechs produce drugs that usefully counteract the bad-effects of other drugs. Often, a new product may seem to work for a while, and then hopes will soar along with stock prices. Again, you need to know how to locate the fine print, because when things don't pan out the related news item will be far less easy to find than the original headline.

There was an interesting moment in April [2000]—a report from Paris of an actual gene therapy victory. The defective immune systems of three infants had been restored using corrected genes. "French Team's Feat Would Be a First," reported the *Washington Post*. The *New York Times* noted that this "first success of gene therapy" had followed "a decade of widely heralded promise followed by dashed hopes." One had lost count of the heralded promises. Now we learned that those hopes had been dashed. All of them. Maybe this one really will work out. It well might—there was no immune system to attack the retrovirus that was used to introduce the repaired genes. But if it doesn't work, you won't read about it on the front page.

Meanwhile, customers beware. The permanent tendency of medical science is to pretend that we know more than we do. Doctors sound silly saying "I don't know." As for journalists, they still can't bring themselves to cast doubt on boastful science.

"Growing numbers of conventionally trained physicians . . . are calling for a 'reinvention' of medical practice to encompass the spiritual."

Spirituality Will Play a Larger Role in Conventional Medicine

Michael S. Goldstein

In the following viewpoint, Michael S. Goldstein asserts that spirituality is becoming an important element of conventional medicine. He contends that medical schools and conventionally trained physicians have begun to study and embrace the healing powers of prayer and other religious practices. However, he also maintains that many issues, such as whether government funds can be used to pay for these treatments and how to evaluate the effectiveness of spiritual care, need to be addressed before spirituality can be fully integrated into conventional medicine. Goldstein is a professor at UCLA's School of Public Health and the author of *Alternative Health Care: Medicine, Miracle, or Mirage?*, the source of the following viewpoint.

As you read, consider the following questions:
1. What is a "healer," as defined by the author?
2. Why does Goldstein believe that "the integration of spirituality into conventional medicine is far from well established"?
3. According to Goldstein, what are the legal issues that would likely be addressed if spirituality were integrated into mainstream medicine?

What impact will spirituality have on the future of alternative medicine? Will the immense pool of spiritual and religious feeling among the population facilitate the integration of alternative approaches into the medical mainstream? Or will the emphasis upon spirituality prove to be an unbridgeable gap with mainstream medical institutions in the context of a pluralistic, democratic, industrial society?

The Attraction of Spirituality

Clearly, the spiritual dimension that pervades alternative medicine is one of its great strengths and attractions. There is a widespread recognition that healing is facilitated by an element of "magic," along with the application of knowledge about the body, mind, and techniques of therapy. Any healer, or type of healing, that can give a sense of hope and meaning to symptoms and illness will be more apt to succeed than one that cannot. At the very least, it will be well thought of by those who use it. Much of conventional medicine has failed in this regard. A large component of alternative medicine's success has been its ability to offer a sense of spirituality that, for many people, allows some "magic" to enter the healing process. Without its spiritual dimension, alternative medicine would be a vastly different phenomenon. The vital importance of healing as a source of meaning simply cannot be underestimated. [Larry] Dossey put it this way in an exhortation to physicians: "Much of society's disillusionment with modern medicine lies in its failure to acknowledge the importance of meaning in health. . . . The contest between conventional and alternative medicine is not about economics, efficacy, safety, and availability; it is about meaning. . . . No matter how technologically effective modern medicine may be, if it does not honor the place of meaning in illness it may lose the allegiance of those it serves."

Meaning is the central issue in comprehending mind-body interaction. A "healer" is someone who can change consciousness and alter meaning. Consciousness itself, in large measure, is meaning. The absence of meaning, if not the equivalent of illness, promotes and intensifies illness. Throughout history, religion and spirituality have been the major means by which meaning is altered. Conventional medicine and physicians have frequently neglected, forgotten, or rejected this reality. It is this glaring gap, be it one of omission or commission, that offers alternative approaches and practitioners their major point of entry to those who are seriously ill.

A Growing Acceptance of Spirituality

The contemporary practice of conventional medicine is more accepting or at least more open to spirituality and "meaning" within medical practice than it has been in the recent past. The photograph in *Life Magazine* of a healer creating an aura over a patient in surgery, working jointly with a surgeon, . . . is a vivid and dramatic example of this new openness. But, more mundane evidence exists as well. A survey of three hundred family practice physicians found that 99 percent believed a patient's religious beliefs could have a positive effect upon the healing process, and 80 percent believed that prayer and meditation have palliative power. The vast majority of these physicians actively sought to integrate these spiritual elements into their practices. Increasingly such sentiments are finding a response in continuing education programs for physicians. Each year since 1995, the Harvard Medical School's Department of Continuing Education has held a course entitled "Spirituality and Healing in Medicine" that has drawn over a thousand attendees annually. The sessions have included talks on Hindu, Buddhist, Jewish, Catholic, Islamic, Pentecostal, Christian Science, and Seventh Day Adventist healing practices. Many talks are offered by practicing clergy, not academics or scholars. For example, a talk on Christian Science was given by Virginia Harris, chairman of the Christian Science Board of Directors. The course organizer, Dr. Herbert Benson, noted that he now gets five or six calls a week from health maintenance organizations (HMOs) that want to incorporate relaxation and other nontraditional healing techniques into their programs. Benson believes that it is unnecessary to differentiate between psychological and spiritual interventions. He finds about 80 percent of his clients are most comfortable with prayer. "So," he writes, "I found I was teaching prayer."

Growing numbers of conventionally trained physicians, especially those in family or primary care medicine, are calling for a "reinvention" of medical practice to encompass the spiritual. The physician is exhorted to view patients' symptoms or complaints within a perspective that includes a spiritual dimension. The idea of healing is expanded to include restoring a sense of internal balance, increasing awareness, and developing a sense of wholeness and meaning, along with any physiological and symptomatic changes. Thus, healing without spirituality is impossible. As Richard Friedman, a professor of psychiatry and participant at the Harvard Conference noted, "Let me make a prediction. Ten years from now . . . doctors will not only ask for a medical history when you come in, but will routinely ask about your belief system as well." In 1995 only a handful of American medical schools offered formal course work on religion and spirituality. By 1998 over thirty did.

Reasons for Management Interest

Health care managers are interested in spirituality for the bottom-line reason that the market is pushing for more holistic approaches to health care, and thus there has been an increase in the inclusion of alternative and complementary medicines. Because spirituality is a crucial component of holistic care, there is, from a marketing point of view, an increased role for spirituality in health care. A second reason for management interest in spirituality is the need to recognize the pluralistic faiths of people involved in health care. Approaching those faiths from the point of view of spirituality may encourage them without producing tension or proselytizing. Spirituality may be the path of interfaith cooperation without interfaith competition.

Third, recent organizational development theory stresses the need to cultivate soul, or spirit, in the workplace. This inherent dimension of people is particularly necessary in times of change. In order for the overall organization to excel, the organization must nurture the spirit or soul of its people. In faith-based health care, this call for soul in the workplace becomes a way of expressing religious identity.

John Shea, *Park Ridge Center Bulletin*, January/February 1999.

In a way that would have seemed impossible if not bizarre a few years ago, conventional medical researchers are beginning to take up the challenge of integrating spirituality into clinical practice. At Duke University, the Department of Medicine is doing randomized, blind, controlled trials of intercessory prayers for 150 patients undergoing cardiac catheterization. Half the patients in the study are being prayed for by up to 100 strangers in eight religious groups around the world: Moravians, Baptists, Carmelite nuns, Buddhist monks in Nepal and France, Jews in Jerusalem, and others. The researchers will be looking at post-operative pain, recovery time, and many other outcomes.

Spirituality Leads to a Number of Questions

Despite such accounts, the integration of spirituality into conventional medicine is far from well established. Neither is it always considered desirable or feasible, even by those who generally support it. Little is known about whether most conventional practitioners are able to effectively convey spiritual techniques to their clients, or whether the clients will be receptive to their inclusion. It is also difficult to assess whether specific spiritual techniques can be adopted by conventional practitioners without adopting the underlying principles upon which they are based. This is of particular concern with regard to techniques, such as traditional Chinese medicine (TCM), that emerge directly from Taoism and Confucianism. The central tenets of these faiths focus on how to live a balanced life, how to best relate to other people, and how to adopt a "proper" style of life. Can the doctor as moral teacher be integrated into our image of the doctor as purveyor of scientific knowledge and technical intervention? Do clients really want, or will they accept, moral advice in lieu of or alongside diagnoses, prescriptions, and therapy? Dossey has written what amounts to a guide to prayer for people who are sick. He accepts that prayer styles will vary according to one's temperament or personality. But, on the basis of empirical studies (The Spindrift experiments), he advocates "nondirected" prayer (prayer without a specific goal) as more effective. Yet Dossey realizes that the use of nondirected prayer as a response to ill health is difficult for many people. Users may have a hidden agenda such as, "I'll pray nondirectly, but I wouldn't mind a cure." Dossey himself is comfortable with the notion that prayer "works" when it leads to a new understanding of the meaning of life or some other new experience or struggle. But will most patients and physicians feel the same?

A crucial question is to what extent the assumptions of an alternative medicine that values spirituality, god, surrender, inner peace, and a clear (if not necessarily conventional) moral code can be integrated into the world of mainstream medicine that is built upon scientific rationality, emotional and intellectual distance from the client, and economic self interest.

Today, when so much of medicine and health care is intimately tied up with the government, these issues have become increasingly complex. Currently the government, directly or indirectly, pays for more than half of the nation's health care expenditures. This includes Medicaid, Medicare, medical research, public health agencies and hospitals, the Veterans Administration hospitals and clinics, and various tax subsidies. The government is also instrumental in setting standards of care; prioritizing research; paying for medical education; and dealing with the widest range of health emergencies, from floods and other natural disasters to pollution and epidemics. All of this takes place within the constitutionally mandated separation of church and state. Although the precise meaning of "the separation of church and state" is constantly being reinterpreted through the courts, it is difficult to imagine that integrating many of alternative medicine's core beliefs about the role of spirituality into mainstream medicine would go unchallenged. The list of legal and policy issues is long and daunting: Could government funds pay for doctors to "teach" people to pray? Could medical education include instruction in religious belief and prayer? Would prayer be offered for all conditions, or just those that are chronic, terminal, psychosomatic, or unresponsive to standard biomedicine? How might such care be evaluated? Would failure mean that the patient just hadn't prayed "hard enough," or might it be a sign of unworthiness? The integration of spirituality into a given individual's response to illness, or a single provider's response to illness, may be desirable and beneficial. However, the institutionalization of these ideas within the health care system is likely to create intense conflict.

"Online consumers are reinventing health care in their own image."

Cyberspace Is Making Patients More Autonomous

Tom Ferguson

Patients are using the Internet as a way to play a larger role in their own health care, Tom Ferguson asserts in the following viewpoint. Ferguson contends that patients are relying on online self-help communities, rather than doctors, to provide information on their ailments and offer moral support. According to Ferguson, these online resources make patients feel unique and valued, validation they rarely receive from physicians. Ferguson is the editor and publisher of the online health newsletter *Ferguson Report* and an adjunct associate professor of health informatics at the University of Texas Medical Sciences Center in Houston.

As you read, consider the following questions:

1. What do "self-helpers" consider to be the most useful online resource, according to Ferguson?
2. What does the author conclude is the primary desire of online "self-helpers"?
3. According to the Better Health and Medical Forum survey, what percentage of users avoided one or more doctor visits because of information they had received on the forum?

From "Health Care in Cyberspace: Patients Lead a Revolution," by Tom Ferguson, *Futurist*, November/December 1997. Copyright © 1997 by *Futurist*. Reprinted with permission.

P atients—not doctors—are leading a revolution in health care by establishing self-help communities in cyberspace. These online networks—each devoted to a single health-related topic, from AIDS and anxiety to wheat intolerance and yeast infections—provide technical medical information, practical coping tips, emotional support, and online second opinions. And they encourage patients to play a highly responsible role in their own care.

These online support communities are available to anyone with a home computer and a modem. Most are free, and many include volunteer health professionals who are experts on the condition being discussed. Group members may communicate in one of several ways: via an electronic mailing list, on USENET newsgroups, on health forums on America Online and CompuServe, or via the message forums now springing up on many of the more than 25,000 health and medical sites currently available on the World Wide Web.

The veteran online self-helpers of today, who check in with their regular online communities several times a week, suggest the ways that millions of patients may use these resources in the not-too-distant future. They spend much of their time online exchanging experiences, opinions, information, and mutual support with others who share their special health concerns. And online self-helpers frequently create new mailing lists and Web sites.

An Example of Online Support

The list of topics that serve as the focus for these communities does not correspond to the chapters of a medical textbook. Online consumers are reinventing health care in their own image. The groups you'll find online cover topics ranging from depression to gambling addiction, from bereavement to dieting for seniors. The names of the groups often sound more like social clubs than like the standard medical specialties. Some groups meet "live" in a virtual online "room." Others post their messages on a central forum, bulletin board, or newsgroup for others to read at their convenience.

Those in need of support often get a rapid and high-quality response in cyberspace. "Jack in Utah" turned to a death-and-dying support group on CompuServe after his son's accidental death. He poured out his heart, sharing his story and his grief—and received dozens of replies over the following 48 hours.

The group advised him to avoid alcohol and drugs, to continue therapy sessions even though they were quite painful, to seek help through his religious faith, and to make a pact with his wife to be extra kind to each other. Members of his group supplied strong empathy and understanding because they were all dealing with similar issues in their own lives.

When I presented Jack's experience at a medical conference for psychologists and psychiatrists, a group of senior therapists concluded that Jack had probably received better advice and support from the online group than he could have gotten from any health professional. Despite their training and concern, they felt that they would not have been able to help him in such an immediate, compassionate, and practical way. . . .

Beneficial Online Resources

When I asked self-helpers what types of online resources they found most useful, the following ranking emerged:

1. "Responses to my own questions by knowledgeable persons" (either clinicians or self-helpers or both).
2. "Answers to questions asked by other self-helpers like myself" (with knowledgeable answers).
3. "Results of my own searches of the Web and other on-line sources."
4. "Professionally generated 'patient education' materials; e.g., printed pamphlets and articles put up on the Web." (This last item ranked much lower than those above.)

This finding came as a considerable surprise. I had assumed that I would find patients using the Net as a sort of giant medical encyclopedia. Instead, I found them using it to communicate with other people—other patients, their friends and family members, and online health professionals. Most online self-help veterans prefer to get the information they need via ongoing conversations within a caring community of people who share their interests.

Because answers to other self-helpers' questions can be so

useful, many online support networks have developed their own lists of Frequently Asked Questions (FAQs). In many cases, these are exquisite, short textbooks on self-care for a particular health concern.

Sharing Authority with Doctors

The whole trend toward managed care makes it imperative for patients to become shrewd and knowledgeable advocates on their own behalf. There is little question that, for better *and* worse, choice and responsibility—and blame, should alternative remedies go badly—are perceptibly shifting to the patient's side of the examining room. According to a study published last year by Cyber Dialogue *(www.cyberdialogue.com)*, an on-line survey-research group, 44 percent of patients now see their relationship with their doctor as one of shared authority, and one-third see themselves as in charge.

Not that patients value that relationship any less. To the contrary, nearly half of U.S. adults express dissatisfaction with the duration of visits to doctors and with their general inaccessibility. According to Daniel Page, executive director of the Health Commons Institute *(www.maine.com/hci/Welcome. html)*, a nonprofit group that promotes shared, informed medical decision making, the perception that doctors just don't have time for us is right on target: The average physician gives patients 18 seconds to describe what ails them before interrupting and moving on.

At that rate, patients may seek to empower themselves to preserve their dignity, if nothing else. In any case, as they assume an active role in preserving their health and curing their illnesses—in decisions that inevitably, one day, become life-and-death ones—they are going to need all the help they can get.

Lisa Prevost, *Civilization*, June/July 1999.

I was also surprised to find that much of what passes for "patient education" in the clinic gets such a low rating from online self-helpers. When I've asked them about this, they have often dismissively referred to such materials as *shovelware*. While they may grudgingly agree that the best of these "canned" materials may be useful to a relatively unsophisticated consumer—or to anyone first coming to terms with a new diagnosis—they often say that much of what passes for patient education materials ranges from the unintentionally inept to the downright patronizing. It provides only one-way, top-down information that often does not address the client's real concerns. It makes the patient the passive recipient of professionally directed care. More importantly, shovelware presumes that the professional knows what the client wants and needs without asking.

The Wishes of Online Consumers

Activist online consumers do not want to be treated like a stereotyped "patient with condition X." They dislike some of the basic medical language that we professionals take for granted: words like *patient* and *compliance* and *victim* and *doctor's orders*. Self-helpers want to be known and treated as unique individuals. They prefer the online forums, discussions, and mailing lists because these resources give them an opportunity to post their own questions and to receive individualized responses. Posing the problem in this way makes them feel respected and valued, not depersonalized and stereotyped.

I have come to the conclusion that what online self-helpers really want is "information in the context of community." Ideally, this is a community of concerned self-helpers, family members, and experienced clinicians.

Understanding Self-Help Communities

For those with little experience communicating online, the very idea that one might be able to have a meaningful interaction with others—and to even become a member of a community—by exchanging typed messages via computer may sound extremely farfetched. But participants are much more than random assortments of online strangers. By their presence, they have already demonstrated their special concern for the focus topic—be it AIDS, depression, or a desire to lose weight.

Knowing that others within the group are walking on the same path, and have come to give and receive support, helps most online self-helpers feel comfortable sharing even the most intimate feelings. Participants often say they can share feelings on their favorite self-help forums they could never discuss at home—even with their closest friends and family members. And so these groups often become an essential part of their members' social support systems. My colleague Ed Madara, director of the American Self-Help Clearinghouse, which tracks such groups, calls these online networks "support groups in slow motion."

Self-help communities in cyberspace can be roughly divided into three realms: physical health concerns, mental health concerns, and recovery/problems of living. Some online self-help leaders are very ill or seriously disabled. A few are literally communicating from their death beds. When I've asked these seriously ill self-helpers why they are spending their last months helping others, they say that "my work online lets me transform a personal misfortune into a benefit for others. And I'd much rather go through my illness 'talking' with dozens of friends than shut away in a darkened room at the end of a hospital corridor."

No one can deny that there is a lot of inaccurate or mistaken health information in cyberspace and that this can be a hazard for the inexperienced. But most experienced online self-helpers feel that they can tell the bad from the good. As in the off-line world, it is largely a matter of knowing whom to trust—and whom to ask. Members of online support networks can easily get a "second opinion" on any questionable information they find online.

There is little hard data about the economic, physical, and psychological benefits of online self-help resources, but some initial surveys have suggested that such benefits may be substantial. In an informal survey of volunteer users by the Better Health and Medical Forum on America Online, 6% said they had avoided one or more emergency room visits because of information they got on this forum. Twenty-six percent said they had avoided one or more doctor visits, and 65% reported an increased ability to cope with a troublesome medical problem.

I've also discovered that the extent of the online resources for a given medical condition cannot easily be predicted on the basis of the problems usually seen in the clinic. Some conditions are equally well represented both online and in the doctor's office, such as cancer and AIDS. But there are large online communities for problems that doctors rarely see, such as attention deficit disorder, chronic fatigue syndrome, and a variety of recovery-related concerns. And there are surprisingly few online resources for some conditions frequently seen in the clinic, such as heart disease, stroke, high blood pressure, and arthritis. . . .

Health Care Must Change

The shift from Industrial Age medicine to Information Age health care will involve much more than just putting our current patient education pamphlets up on the Web. Thinking that we could simply substitute one medium for another without deep structural changes in our medical infrastructure is like thinking that the shift from the railroad age to the airplane age would simply mean landing all those 747s in Grand Central Station.

We will have arrived at true Information Age health care when we all take it for granted that the primary practitioner in our health care system is the informed, empowered, online layperson. As we move farther into the Information Age, health professionals will do more than just treat their patients' ills—they will increasingly serve as their coaches, teachers, and colleagues, working side-by-side with empowered consumers in a high-quality system of computer-supported, low-cost, self-managed care.

> "The only way to go back to an idealized
> view of the physician-patient relationship
> would be to roll back the development of
> scientific medicine."

The Traditional Physician-Patient Relationship Is Becoming Obsolete

Kevin W. Wildes

In the following viewpoint, Kevin W. Wildes argues that the traditional patient-physician relationship is becoming obsolete as scientific medicine evolves. According to Wildes, physicians were once seen as being better suited than their patients to make health care decisions. However, today, patients are better able to make informed health care decisions for themselves. Wildes concludes that the traditional patient-physician relationship will likely be replaced with newer models that recognize patient autonomy. Wildes is an associate professor of philosophy at Georgetown University in the District of Columbia.

As you read, consider the following questions:
1. How does Wildes define the older model of medicine?
2. According to the author, why has contemporary medicine been able to help people?
3. In Wildes's opinion, what is the strength of the consumer model for patient-physician relationships?

At a recent conference on managed care, one of the speakers, a physician, complained that all too often we don't call patients "patients" any more. These days patients are referred to as either customers, consumers, clients or covered lives. As is often the case at such physician meetings, the statement on nomenclature received a lot of support, and there was nostalgia for the "golden days" of medicine. But there was no serious reflection about what the language changes may signify or about the nature of the changes in medicine.

Why did the golden age collapse? Was it as golden as some remember?

Medical Nostalgia

On first reflection, the change in language may be taken as a symptom of the central role that economics has come to play in the practice of medicine. The shift in language, however, indicates something far more profound than changes in health care finance. The struggle over the language of medicine reflects a deeper crisis about the purpose and role of medicine in our society. If one thinks about this crisis and its roots, one comes to realize that there can be no return to some past time, no matter how much that past is idealized. Nor is such a return desirable.

In the current crisis an older model of medicine, which focuses on the patient-physician relationship, is often romanticized. This older model, rooted in the traditions of Hippocratic medicine, empowers the physician to act on behalf of the patient. The model is described as a fiduciary relationship, in which the physician is an advocate for the good of the patient. In the American imagination, this view of the past evokes images of a Norman Rockwell painting. People imagine the physician and the patient alone in the doctor's examination room, where the patient could reveal his or her fears or deepest concerns. The nostalgia for the golden days of medicine assumes that if we could only get the insurers out of the picture, or at least out of the clinic, everything would be fine. But this is not the case.

These Rockwellian images are woefully inadequate and inappropriate. Like it or not, we have come to desire the curing and technological interventions of modern medicine that have been shaped by the merger of clinic and laboratory. The development and application of basic scientific knowledge have led to advances in diagnosis and treatment that we have come to expect from medicine. As a result of these advances, we now expect medicine to cure people. This expectation is a significant change in understanding its purpose and goals. For most of history, people hoped that medicine might ameliorate their conditions and problems, but they did not expect physicians would actually cure them. If patients recovered health, it was a miracle.

A Complicated Relationship

The move to scientific medicine inevitably reshaped the patient-physician relationship. Medical knowledge is based on probabilities. Scientific knowledge in medicine is based, not on knowledge about individual patients, but on knowledge about populations of patients. Contemporary medicine has been able to help people because it has studied the health of populations and it uses that model of knowledge to guide the treatment of particular patients. It is this development of knowledge that has enabled contemporary medicine to develop the technical and medical interventions that work the "miracles" that have become commonplace. These miracles come from the application of scientific knowledge, not from divine intervention. The development of scientific medicine crowds out religious language from the clinical experience. And as Eric Cassells points out, scientific medicine follows a Cartesian model of the person, focusing on the body as a machine. The emphasis of the scientific-medical approach is to fix the machine when it is broken.

The patient-physician relationship is further complicated by the need of scientific medicine for a significant investment of resources and infrastructure support. Because of the need for organizational support, modern medicine has developed a bureaucratic culture that plays an essential part in the delivery of health care. Each of these developments further complicates the physician-patient relationship. Even in the Golden Age there were a lot of people in the clinic. Rockwell should have included basic scientists, nurses, financiers and administrators along with the physician and the patient.

Contemporary medicine now finds itself in a crisis about what it is and what it should be. Some may wish to return to the Rockwell-style physician-patient relationship. But this is not possible if one wants to maintain the advances of scientific medicine. Even if such a return were possible, it would be undesirable for at least three reasons. First, the traditional Hippocratic view of patients was extraordinarily paternalistic, though this paternalism was often covered over with the language of a fiduciary relationship. In the Hippocratic Oath the physician swears to act in the best interests of the patient according to the physician's judgment. However, over the last 40 years we have come to understand that the physician's view of the patient's best interest and the patient's view of his or her best interest may often be quite different.

A second reason not to romanticize the past is that the model of being a patient, overcome by disease, fails to take into account a great deal that we now know about disease prevention and health promotion. The patient model does not seriously address the responsibility people have for their own health. In the older model patients are simply overcome by illness, and there is no place for individual responsibility or choice in how the sickness occurred. We now know that many illnesses and diseases are brought on by the lifestyle choices of men and women. The older model often leads to the infantilization of the patient.

Finally, because of the view of illness as overtaking the patient, the older model led to modern medicine's focus on acute care. In general, the patient only went to see the physician when something was wrong. The overall emphasis in our medical and health care system was on fixing the parts of the machine that are broken, not on preventing the breakdown.

New Models for Medicine

The older model does not work from another perspective. It cannot account for medicine as a social enterprise, since it too narrowly focuses on the individual patient. The development of scientific medicine has opened up all kinds of new treatment possibilities for men and women. These possibilities raise important moral and economic questions about how we deploy health care resources. The question of cost containment and resource allocation is a moral question as well as an economic one. In a world of limited resources, how a society stewards its resources is a moral question. But the older Hippocratic ethic is incapable, conceptually, of addressing the questions of allocating health care resources (as Alan Buchanan argued in an issue of the *Kennedy Institute of Ethics Journal*). Nor can the older physician ethic incorporate other social questions, such as who has access to the system. The Hippocratic tradition is focused only on the patient, in a paternalistic way. The tradition does not have a social ethic. Yet contemporary medicine is a social enterprise.

The Consumer Model Will Benefit Family Physicians

Consumerism poses a significant adaptive challenge for health care providers. However, the trend also carries with it a silver lining of opportunity for family physicians. With increasing patient access and share-of-cost, health care is becoming a "balanced" consumer model, in which end users bear significant accountability for the cost of purchased goods and services.

This power should translate into additional compensation for responsiveness, access, empathy and communication. Under prepaid managed care, primary care physicians typically receive the capitation rate, regardless of their individual levels of service excellence. Under a balanced consumer model, family physicians have the opportunity to gain additional rewards for total patient satisfaction. As the balanced consumer model takes hold, patients will bear more and more costs and be increasingly responsible for defining health care value. This consolidated power should eventually translate into additional physician compensation for responsiveness, access, empathy and communication—special attributes in which family physicians take great pride.

Norman E. Vinn, *Family Practice Management*, January 2000.

There are at least two other models in which to frame the patient-physician relationship. One is the market model, in which the patient is seen as an informed consumer. This is a model we have flirted with, but have not really tried, in the United States. In spite of all of the contemporary language about markets, individuals are not true consumers in our current health insurance system. The major choices in health care are made not by individuals but by human resource officers and benefits managers who decide which plan(s) will be available to employees. But employees are not true consumers, as they are not empowered to shop for health care. So one approach would be to develop and try a true market model for medicine, in which individuals are understood to be informed consumers. Another model is the political model. Here health care is less a business and more a community. This is a model that stresses health care as part of the common good, the importance of all parties having a voice and considerations of public health. Both models present possible ways to re-imagine and redefine medicine.

I would argue that while each model contains some good insights, neither model is fully appropriate for contemporary health care. If one builds upon the insights from these models, it is possible to begin to develop a new model for the patient. The strength of the community-based model is that it understands there are communal obligations to provide health care for men and women. The weakness of the model turns on its strength: the idea of community.

The first problem with the community model is that secular societies are not themselves communities, though they are often collections of communities. Furthermore, ideas about health, disease and health care are often interpreted by the values of a community. The difficulty with using the community model is that there will be differing views of health care depending on the model of community deployed. We are left with the question, to paraphrase [philosopher] Alasdair MacIntyre: "Whose community? Which health care?" We have no way, in a secular society, to decide which model of community and health is the one we should use.

The strength of the consumer model is that it allows freedom of choice. It allows the individual the liberty to make health care choices appropriate to the person's own life and moral commitments. The consumer model is a procedural way to avoid the interminable debates about what should or should not be included in packages of health care. I believe it is possible to bring these models together. We can argue that society is obliged to provide basic access to health care for all citizens, but it must structure this in a way that allows individuals freedom to make their own health care decisions. Here one might think of a system of vouchers for health care.

Determining the Purpose of Medicine

It is clear that medicine has changed and there is no going back. Indeed, the only way to go back to an idealized view of the physician-patient relationship would be to roll back the development of scientific medicine. Few would want to do that. The real crisis before us is to determine the purpose or purposes of medicine in our society. Such a determination can take place only in open discussions within a free, democratic society.

Periodical Bibliography

The following articles have been selected to supplement the diverse views presented in this chapter.

American Medical News	"Creating a Cyber Doctor-Patient Relationship," August 6, 2001.
Tony Blankley	"Technology Creates Moral Ambiguities," *Conservative Chronicle*, September 5, 2001.
Larry R. Churchill	"We Are Our Genes—Not!" *World & I*, November 2001.
Victoria Stagg Elliott	"Doctor Roboto," *American Medical News*, November 20, 2000.
Francis Fukuyama	"The House Was Right to Ban Cloning," *Wall Street Journal*, August 2, 2001.
Eric S. Grace	"Better Health Through Gene Therapy," *Futurist*, January/February 1998.
William A. Haseltine	"Regenerative Medicine," *New Perspectives Quarterly*, Summer 2000.
Carol P. Herbert	"The Future of Family Medicine: Research," *Journal of Family Practice*, July 2001.
Leon R. Kass	"Preventing a Brave New World," *Human Life Review*, Summer 2001.
Gina Kolata	"In Cloning, Failure Far Exceeds Success," *New York Times*, December 11, 2001.
Richard Powers	"Too Many Breakthroughs," *New York Times*, November 19, 1998.
Christoph Rehmann-Sutter	"Liberating Gene Therapy?" *Hastings Center Report*, May/June 1999.
Stephen J. Russell	"Gene Therapy," *British Medical Journal*, November 15, 1997.
Joan Stephenson	"Studies Illuminate Cause of Fatal Reaction in Gene-Therapy Trial," *Journal of the American Medical Association*, May 23, 2001.
Gregory Stock	"A Tempest in a Petri Dish," *Los Angeles Times*, December 2, 2001.
Larry Thompson	"Human Gene Therapy: Harsh Lessons, High Hopes," *FDA Consumer*, September/October 2000.

For Further Discussion

Chapter 1

1. The authors in this chapter evaluated several problems with the American medical system. Which of those problems do you think is the most serious? Are there other issues, outside the ones discussed in the viewpoints, that you think significantly affect the quality of American medicine? Explain your answers.

2. Suzanne Gordon maintains that health maintenance organizations have lessened the quality of American medicine by discouraging doctors from treating sick patients. However, Thomas W. Hazlett asserts that HMOs have improved health care and made it more affordable. Which argument do you find more valid and why?

3. In its viewpoint, the Quality Interagency Coordination Task Force explains the extent of and reasons for fatal medical errors. What steps do you think should be taken to reduce these mistakes? Explain your answer.

Chapter 2

1. The National Institutes of Health is overseen by the Department of Health and Human Services. Stephen Barrett is the vice president of the National Council Against Health Fraud and a scientific adviser to the American Council on Science and Health. Based on their respective credentials, whose argument on the benefits of acupuncture do you find more convincing? Why?

2. Homeopathic medicine is based on the theory that diseases can be cured if patients are given minute doses of natural substances that in larger quantities would produce symptoms of the disease being treated. Rudolph Ballentine and David W. Ramey disagree about homeopathy's effectiveness. After reading their viewpoints, do you think that homeopathy is beneficial or harmful? Why?

3. One of the major arguments against alternative medicine is that such treatments have not been adequately tested for their efficacy and safety. However, proponents of alternative treatments argue that the use of these treatments for thousands of years in non-western medicine proves their benefits. Do you believe that government agencies should examine alternative treatments more closely, or is such testing an indication of the lack of respect given to non-Western health care? Explain your answers.

Chapter 3

1. According to Peggy Slasman, pigs and other animals can safely provide organs for humans in need of transplants. Assuming that xenotransplantations can be performed successfully and do not pose health risks to the patients, do you believe it is ethical for animals to be used as organ donors? Why or why not?

2. Sarah Scott and Roger Gosden disagree over whether women in their forties and fifties should make use of reproductive technologies. Whose argument do you find more convincing? Please explain.

3. After reading the viewpoints by Richard Cohen and William Norman Grigg, what is your opinion on President George W. Bush's decision to limit embryonic stem cell research? Do you believe that limiting research is unethical because it could prevent medical breakthroughs that could save numerous lives, or are greater restrictions on stem cell research advisable because they protect the right of the individual? Explain your answer.

Chapter 4

1. In his viewpoint, G. Terry Sharrer acknowledges that while genetic cures will increase life expectancy and improve the quality of life for many patients, the "original concept of gene therapy" has been largely unsuccessful. Tom Bethell also observes that gene therapy has yet to be proven effective. Given those caveats, do you think that genetic cures will change medicine? Why or why not?

2. Michael S. Goldstein, Tom Ferguson, and Kevin W. Wildes contend that the relationship between patients and doctors is evolving, as patients turn to other sources, such as spirituality and the Internet, to better understand their illnesses and possible treatments. What is your opinion on the increased autonomy of patients? Does this independence help or hinder the quality of care that doctors can provide? Explain your answer.

3. The American medical system has changed significantly in recent decades. Which of the viewpoints in this chapter do you think best depicts how American medicine will continue to evolve? What other issues do you believe will affect the future of medicine? Explain your answer.

Organizations to Contact

The editors have compiled the following list of organizations concerned with the issues debated in this book. The descriptions are derived from materials provided by the organizations. All have publications or information available for interested readers. The list was compiled on the date of publication of the present volume; the information provided here may change. Be aware that many organizations take several weeks or longer to respond to inquiries, so allow as much time as possible.

American Council on Science and Health (ACSH)
1995 Broadway, 2nd Fl., New York, NY 10023-5860
(212) 362-7044 • fax: (212) 362-4919
e-mail: acsh@acsh.org • website: www.acsh.org

ACSH is a consumer education group concerned with issues related to food, nutrition, chemicals, pharmaceuticals, lifestyle, the environment, and health. It publishes the quarterly newsletter *Priorities* as well as the report *Biotech Pharmaceuticals and Biotherapy*.

American Holistic Medical Association (AHMA)
6728 McLean Village Drive, McLean, VA 22101-8729
Fax: (703) 556-8729
e-mail: info@holisticmedicine.org
website: www.holisticmedicine.org

AHMA promotes the practice of holistic health care, a concept that emphasizes the integration of physical, mental, emotional, and spiritual concerns with environmental harmony. It publishes a quarterly newsletter.

American Medical Association (AMA)
515 N. State St., Chicago, IL 60610
(312) 464-5000
website: www.ama-assn.org

AMA is the largest professional association for medical doctors. It helps set standards for medical education and practices, and it is a powerful lobby in Washington for physicians' interests. The association publishes journals for many medical fields, including the monthly *Archives of Surgery* and the weekly *JAMA*.

American Public Health Association (APHA)
800 I St. NW, Washington, DC 20001-3710
(202) 777-APHA • fax: (202) 777-2534
e-mail: comments@apha.org • website: www.apha.org

Founded in 1872, the American Public Health Association consists of over 50,000 individuals and organizations that aim to improve public health. Its members represent over fifty public health occupations, including researchers, practitioners, administrators, teachers, and other health care workers. Some of APHA's publications include the monthly *American Journal of Public Health* and the books *Case Studies in Public Health Ethics* and *Health and Welfare for Families in the 21st Century*.

American Society for Reproductive Medicine (ASRM)
1209 Montgomery Hwy., Birmingham, AL 35216
(205) 978-5000 • fax: (205) 978-5005
e-mail: asrm@asrm.org • website: www.asrm.org

Established in 1944, ASRM is a voluntary, nonprofit organization devoted to advancing knowledge and expertise in reproductive medicine and biology. Its members include obstetricians, gynecologists, nurses, and research scientists. The society publishes the journal *Fertility and Sterility*, the newsletters *ASRM News* and *Menopausal Medicine*, and booklets on reproductive medicine. The ASRM Ethics Committee issues policy statements on the responsible use of reproductive technologies.

American Society of Law, Medicine & Ethics (ASLME)
765 Commonwealth Ave., Suite 1634, Boston, MA 02215
(617) 262-4990 • fax: (617) 437-7596
e-mail: info@aslme.org • website: www.aslme.org

The ASLME aims to provide high-quality scholarship and debate to professionals in the fields of law, health care, policy, and ethics. The society acts as a source of guidance and information through the publication of two quarterlies, the *Journal of Law, Medicine & Ethics* and the *American Journal of Law & Medicine*.

Center for Bioethics
University of Pennsylvania
3401 Market St. #320, Philadelphia, PA 19104
(215) 898-7136 • fax: (215) 573-3036
e-mail: mcgee@mail.med.upenn.edu
website: www.uphs.upenn.edu

The Center of Bioethics at the University of Pennsylvania is the largest bioethics center in the world, and it runs the world's first and largest bioethics website. Faculty at the center conduct research on issues including human research and experimentation, genetic testing, and transplantation. *PennBioethics* is its quarterly newsletter.

Center for Disease Control—Office of Genetics and Disease Prevention (OGDP)
4770 Buford Hwy., Mailstop K28, Atlanta, GA 30341-3724
(770) 488-3235 • fax: (770) 488-3236
e-mail: genetics@cdc.gov • website: www.cdc.gov

The purpose of the Office of Genetics and Disease Prevention is to provide a coordinated focus for CDC-wide, cross-cutting genetics efforts and to raise awareness of genetics and disease prevention. It has published the reports *Ethical and Social Issues in the Use of Biomarkers in Epidemiological Research* and *Informed Consent for Stored Tissue Samples*.

Council for Responsible Genetics
5 Upland Rd., Suite 3, Cambridge, MA 02140
(617) 868-0870 • fax: (617) 491-5344
e-mail: crg@gene-watch.org • website: www.gene-watch.org

The council is a national organization of scientists, health professionals, trade unionists, women's health activists, and others who work to ensure that biotechnology is developed safely and in the public interest. The council publishes the bimonthly magazine *GeneWatch*, position papers on the Human Genome Project, genetic discrimination, germ-line modifications, and DNA-based identification systems, and the book *Exploding the Gene Myth*.

The Hastings Center
Route 9D, Garrison, NY 10524-5555
(914) 424-4040 • fax: (914) 424-4545
e-mail: mail@thehastingscenter.org
website: www.hastingscenter.org

The Hastings Center is an independent research institute that explores the medical, ethical, and social ramifications of biomedical advances. The center publishes books, papers, guidelines, and the bimonthly *Hastings Center Report*.

Healthcare Leadership Council (HLC)
900 17th St. NW, Suite 600, Washington, DC 20006
(202) 452-8700
website: www.hlc.org

The council is a forum in which health care industry leaders can jointly develop policies, plans, and programs that support a market-based health care system. HLC believes America's health care system should value innovation and provide affordable high-quality health care free from excessive government regulations. It offers the latest press releases on health issues and several public policy papers with titles such as "Empowering Consumers and Patients" and "Ensuring Responsible Government."

Kennedy Institute of Ethics
Georgetown University
1437 37th St. NW, Washington, DC 20057
(202) 687-8099 • library: (800) 633-3849 • fax: (202) 687-6779

The institute sponsors research on medical ethics, including ethical issues surrounding the use of recombinant DNA and human gene therapy. It supplies the National Library of Medicine with an online database on bioethics and publishes an annual bibliography in addition to reports and articles on specific issues concerning medical ethics.

Living Bank
PO Box 6725, Houston, TX 77265
(713) 528-2971 • fax: (713) 961-0979 • hot line: (800) 528-2971
e-mail: jeiche@livingbank.org • website: www.livingbank.org

The bank is an international registry and referral service for people wishing to donate organs and/or tissue for transplantation, therapy, or research. Its volunteers speak to civic organizations about the benefits of organ donation, and its 350,000-donor population spreads through fifty states and sixty-three foreign countries. It provides educational materials on organ donation and publishes a bimonthly newsletter, the *Living Banker*.

National Bioethics Advisory Commission (NBAC)
6100 Executive Boulevard, Suite 5B01, Rockville, MD
20892-7508
(301) 402-4242 • fax: (301) 480-6900
e-mail: info@bioethics.gov • website: www.bioethics.gov

NBAC is a federal agency that sets guidelines that govern the ethical conduct of research. It works to protect the rights and welfare of human research subjects and govern the management and use of genetic information. Its published reports include *Research Involving Persons with Mental Disorders That May Affect Decision-making Capacity* and *Cloning Human Beings*.

National Center for Complementary and Alternative Medicine (NCCAM)
PO Box 7923, Gaithersburg, MD 20898
(301) 519-3153 • fax: (866) 464-3616
e-mail: info@nccam.nih.gov • website: http://nccam.nih.gov

Congress established the NCCAM in 1998 to encourage and support research on complementary and alternative medicine (CAM). The center also provides information on CAM to health care providers and the public, evaluates the safety and effectiveness of popular herbal remedies and practices such as acupuncture, and supports studies to determine how CAM products interact with standard medications. NCCAM publishes consensus reports and fact sheets on various alternative treatments, cancer, and dietary supplements.

National Coalition on Health Care

555 13th St. NW, Washington, DC 20004
(202) 637-6830 • fax: (202) 637-6861
website: www.nchc.org

The National Coalition on Health Care is a nonprofit, nonpartisan group that represents the nation's largest alliance working to improve America's health care and make it more affordable. The coalition offers several policy studies with titles ranging from "Why the Quality of U.S. Health Care Must Be Improved" to "The Rising Number of Uninsured Workers: An Approaching Crisis in Health Care Financing."

National Institutes of Health (NIH)

Bethesda, MD 20892
(301) 496-4000
e-mail: nihinfo@od.nih.gov • website: www.nih.gov

The NIH is comprised of twenty-seven separate components, including the National Human Genome Research Institute, and the National Cancer Institute. Its mission is to discover new knowledge that will improve everyone's health. In order to achieve this mission, the NIH conducts and supports research, helps train research investigators, and fosters the communication of medical information. The NIH also publishes online fact sheets, brochures, and handbooks.

National Women's Health Information Center (NWHIC)

8550 Arlington Blvd., Suite 300, Fairfax, VA 22031
(800) 994-9662
website: www.4woman.gov

The NWHIC is a service of the Office on Women's Health in the Department of Health and Human Services. It provides access to current and reliable information on a wide array of women's health issues. The organization publishes a monthly newsletter, *Healthy Women Today*.

Quackwatch
PO Box 1747, Allentown, PA 18105
(610) 437-1795
e-mail: sbinfo@quackwatch.com • website: www.quackwatch.com

Quackwatch is a nonprofit corporation that combats health-related frauds and fads. Its activities include reporting illegal marketing of medical-related products, improving the quality of health information available on the Internet, and distributing reliable publications. The website has reports on topics including herbal medicine, homeopathy, and other alternative treatments.

Transplantation Society
Central Business Office
205 Viger Avenue West, Suite 201, Montreal, QC,
Canada H2Z 1G2
(514) 874-1998 • fax: (514) 874-1580
e-mail: info@transplantation-soc.org
website: www.transplantation-soc.org

The Transplantation Society works to increase and promote information about transplantation. It is composed of physicians and scientists who have made significant contributions to the advancement of knowledge in transplantation biology and medicine. The society publishes the *Transplantation Society Bulletin* annually.

United Network for Organ Sharing (UNOS)
1100 Boulders Parkway, Suite 500, PO Box 13770, Richmond,
VA 23225-8770
(804) 330-8500 • fax: (804) 330-8507
website: www.unos.org

UNOS is a system of transplant and organ procurement centers, tissue-typing labs, and transplant surgical teams. It was formed to help organ donors and people who need organs to find each other. By federal law, organs used for transplants must be cleared through UNOS. The network also formulates and implements national policies on equal access to organs and organ allocation, organ procurement, and AIDS testing. It publishes the monthly *UNOS Update*.

Bibliography of Books

Jean-Marie Abgrall — *Healing or Stealing?: Medical Charlatans in the New Age.* New York: Algora, 2000.

Bryan Appleyard — *Brave New Worlds: Staying Human in the Genetic Future.* New York: Viking, 1998.

Rudolph Ballentine — *Radical Healing.* New York: Three Rivers Press, 1999.

Daniel Callahan — *False Hopes: Why America's Quest for Perfect Health Is a Recipe for Failure.* New York: Simon and Schuster, 1998.

Anne Donchin and Laura M. Purdy, eds. — *Embodying Bioethics: Recent Feminist Advances.* Lanham, MD: Rowman & Littlefield, 1999.

Larry Dossey — *Reinventing Medicine: Beyond Mind-Body to a New Era of Healing.* San Francisco: HarperSanFrancisco, 1999.

Jacalyn Duffin — *History of Medicine: A Scandalously Short Introduction.* Toronto: University of Toronto Press, 1999.

Richard Epstein — *Mortal Peril: Our Inalienable Right to Health Care?* Reading, MA: Addison-Wesley, 1997.

Leo Galland — *The Four Pillars of Healing.* New York: Random House, 1997.

Bernard Gert, Charles M. Culver, and K. Donner Clouser — *Bioethics: A Return to Fundamentals.* New York: Oxford University Press, 1997.

Michael S. Goldstein — *Alternative Health Care: Medicine, Miracle, or Mirage?* Philadelphia: Temple University Press, 1999.

James S. Gordon — *Holistic Medicine.* Philadelphia: Chelsea House, 2001.

Rena J. Gordon, Barbara Cable Nienstedt, and Wilbert M. Gesler, eds. — *Alternative Therapies: Expanding Options in Health Care.* New York: Springer, 1998.

Roger Gosden — *Designing Babies: The Brave New World of Reproductive Technology.* New York: W.H. Freeman, 1999.

Martin L. Gross — *The Medical Racket: How Doctors, HMOs, and Hospitals Are Failing the American Patient.* New York: Avon Books, 1998.

Elisabeth Hildt and Sigrid Graumann, eds. — *Genetics in Human Reproduction.* Aldershot, UK: Ashgate, 1999.

Albert R. Jonsen   *The Birth of Bioethics*. New York: Oxford University Press, 1998.

Tamara Kohn and   *Extending the Boundaries of Care: Medical Ethics*
Rosemary McKechnie,   *and Caring Practices*. Oxford, UK: Berg,
eds.   1999.

Gina Kolata   *Cloning: The Road to Dolly and the Path Ahead*. New York: William Morrow, 1998.

Paul Lauritzen, ed.   *Cloning and the Future of Human Embryo Research*. Oxford, UK: Oxford University Press, 2001.

James Marti   *The Alternative Health & Medicine Encyclopedia*. Detroit: Gale Research, 1998.

Gary E. McCuen   *Cloning: Science & Society*. Hudson, WI: GEM, 1998.

Jonathan D. Moreno   *Undue Risk: Secret State Experiments on Humans*. New York: W.H. Freeman, 2000.

Lawrence J. O'Brien   *Bad Medicine: How the American Medical Establishment Is Ruining Our Healthcare System*. Amherst, NY: Prometheus Books, 1999.

OECD   *Xenotransplantation: International Policy Issues*. Paris: Organisation for Economic Co-operation and Development, 1999.

Gregory E. Pence   *Re-creating Medicine: Ethical Issues at the Frontiers of Medicine*. Lanham, MD: Rowman & Littlefield, 2000.

Sally Satel   *PC, M.D.: How Political Correctness Is Corrupting Medicine*. New York: Basic Books, 2000.

William B. Schwartz   *Life Without Disease: The Pursuit of Medical Utopia*. Berkeley: University of California Press, 1998.

Victor S. Sierpina   *Integrative Health Care: Complementary and Alternative Therapies for the Whole Person*. Philadelphia: F.A. Davis, 2001.

Lawrence Tyler   *Understanding Alternative Medicine: New Health Paths in America*. New York: Haworth Herbal Press, 2000.

Robert M. Veatch, ed.   *Cross-Cultural Perspectives in Medical Ethics*. Boston: Jones and Bartlett, 2000.

Kenman L. Wong   *Medicine and the Marketplace: The Moral Dimensions of Managed Care*. South Bend, IN: University of Notre Dame Press, 1998.

Index